HOW TO INVEST

IN

REAL ESTATE

With as Little as $1,000

NANCY DUNNAN

PERENNIAL LIBRARY

Harper & Row, Publishers, New York
Cambridge, Philadelphia, San Francisco, Washington
London, Mexico City, São Paulo, Singapore, Sydney

This book is sold with the understanding that neither the Author nor the Publisher is engaged in rendering legal or financial services. As each situation is unique, questions relevant to the practice of law or personal finance and specific to the individual should be addressed to a member of those professions to ensure that the situation has been evaluated carefully and appropriately.

The Author and Publisher specifically disclaim any liability, loss, or risk, personal or otherwise, which is incurred as a consequence, directly or indirectly, of the use and application of any of the contents of this work.

HOW TO INVEST IN REAL ESTATE. Copyright © 1987 by Cloverdale Press, Inc. All rights reserved. Printed in the United States of America. No part of this book may be used or reproduced in any manner whatsoever without written permission except in the case of brief quotations embodied in critical articles and reviews. For information address Harper & Row, Publishers, Inc., 10 East 53rd Street, New York, N.Y. 10022.

First edition published 1987.

Produced by Cloverdale Press, Inc., 133 Fifth Avenue, New York, N.Y. 10003.

Library of Congress Cataloging-in-Publication Data

Dunnan, Nancy.
How to invest in real estate with as little as $1,000.

(Smart money series)
1. Real estate investment.   I. Title.
HD1382.5.D86   1987   332.63'24   86-45648
ISBN 0-06-096042-6 (pbk.)
87 88 89 90 91 MPC 10 9 8 7 6 5 4 3 2 1

CONTENTS

PART ONE

Home
Sweet Home

Introduction

From early wigwam to stately Colonial, from humble log cabin to elaborate Victorian, Americans have always been romantically involved with shelter. Ever since the first saltbox made its appearance on the rugged coast of New England, and wagon trains of pioneers staked their claims to the prairies of the Midwest, real estate has intrigued each succeeding generation.

Real estate as we know it today has evolved from those early settlements to a vast and varied field of investment that's accessible to one and all. And, as you will see, the financial and personal pleasures that traditionally accompany real estate can be yours, whether you have $1,000 or $10,000 or $100,000 to invest.

In fact, real estate knows no boundaries and can be found anywhere, at any price, and in any size, ranging from a rented room or a manufactured home to a posh fifteen-room co-op to shares in a well-run real estate trust. The opportunities surround all of us—you have only to look, learn, and then act decisively in order to profit handsomely.

Since the mid-1970's, real estate's dual attraction of appreciation and tax shelter have made it a continual winner. During the past ten years, the average price of a single-family home has increased 213 percent. Furthermore, numerous studies indicate that real estate investments continually beat the stock market, over the long term.

Buying a Co-op or Condominium. Thousands of Americans have become cooperative and condominium owners with remarkable success. Co-op prices in New York City, for example, have generally increased drastically over the past decade, rising in many cases to the one-million-dollar mark. Across the nation, similar if less spectacular price increases have occurred. You'll learn how to judge the market, time your purchase or sale, and avoid the pitfalls. In addition, MORTGAGES & CREATIVE FINANCING (see Chapter 24) explains how to get the most dollars at the best rates, how to talk to bankers, and how to refinance.

Renting Out a Room. Maybe you never realized it, but you have rentable property right in your own home or apartment. That spare guest room can easily be turned into a steady income-producer. And, once you get a taste of the sweet monetary rewards you'll be ready to expand and find other rentable property you can manage.

Bed & Breakfast. Renting out one or two rooms can be turned into a remarkably profitable business if you offer not only beds but blueberry muffins and coffee, too. In a world where hotels charge $50 to $200 per night, there is plenty of opportunity for the astute real estate investor in you to compete—and make excellent profits.

Vacation Homes. Whether a weekend retreat in the country, a ski house in the mountains, or a cottage on the lake, vacation homes have always been part of everyone's dream, and now one can be yours—for much less than you think. Chapters 12 and 13 detail the ins and outs of vacation home ownership and time sharing.

Buying With a Friend. If you've always thought real estate investments were beyond the limits of your pocketbook, you'll delight in discovering the joys of buying property with a friend or partner. You'll learn exactly how to go about it, how to find the right lawyer, and what type of contract to sign.

The New Tax Law

The 1986 Tax Reform Act was basically kind to homeowners but tough on investors in real estate tax shelters. Those shelters previously geared to generating huge tax write-offs have been eliminated, and in general, investors should look now for income-producing investments. However, by understanding the new regulations and making timely investments, you can come out relatively unscathed. Here are the key factors to keep in mind.

Primary Residences: 1) You are still able to deduct your mortgage interest payments and interest paid on home improvement loans, up to the cost of the home, as well as property taxes on your principal residence. In addition, interest on a mortgage used to finance the cost of home improvements is also deductible; **2)** Interest on home equity loans and second mortgages is still deductible up to the purchase price of the home and cost of any improvements, less any first mortgage indebtedness; **3)** Any gain made when you sell your primary residence remains currently excludible, provided you buy another home of equal or greater value within certain time frames; **4)** If you're 55 or older, you can still take the once-in-a-lifetime exemption from taxes on up to $125,000 of gains made from the sale of your home.

Vacation and Second Homes. Mortgage interest payments and property tax remain fully deductible on a second home as long as you personally use it at least 14 days a year or a period of time that's at least 10 percent as long as the time rented, whichever is more. You must report this rental income, but you can write off rental expenses, such as maintenance, repairs, insurance, utilities, and depreciation. These deductions are generally limited to the amount of your rental income. (If you rent it out 14 days or less, you are not required to report the rental income, nor can you deduct expenses.)

Rental Property. Owners who actively manage rental property can deduct up to $25,000 in losses against other income *if* their income is $100,000 or less. Special rules apply to renting out vacation homes for more than 14 days. (See Chapter 12 for details.)

Depreciation. Depreciation of rental property has been changed. Prior to the Tax Reform Act of 1986 you could depreciate residential and commercial rental property over 19 years. Now it's been stretched out over 27.5 years for residential rental property and 31 years for commercial rental property; this means the dollar amount you can write off is reduced each year.

Passive Investments. Many real estate investments, including most limited partnerships, were originally designed as tax shelters with "passive" or "paper" losses which could be used to offset other income (salary, dividends, interest income, etc.) from taxes. Now, these losses can *only* be used to offset passive income from other passive (including real estate) activities. Consequently, investors should seek investments that generate true income rather than paper losses. It is important to note that passive losses in one year may be carried forward to offset passive income in future years.

Phase-out rules may affect all of these things during the transition period between the old and new tax laws. Be sure to check with your accountant as to how phase-out rules could impact any planned real estate investment.

To get your start on the road to real estate riches, take a look at the Table of Contents. Select one or two of the most appealing topics and read those chapters first. By arming yourself with accurate data and selecting real estate investments that match your pocketbook and your appetite for risk, you'll find it surprisingly easy to become a happy and successful real estate mogul.

Buying a House

Today, with real estate at an all-time high, owning one's own home continues to be the cornerstone of the American dream. Yet inflation and our growing population have pushed prices of houses and apartments higher and higher, to such a level, in fact, that many Americans think they're locked out of the action. Perhaps you, too, feel as though everyone—everyone but you, that is—has made a fortune in real estate. Perhaps you cringe when you hear friends and friends of friends brag that they bought their homes when prices were much lower and that now they've doubled or even tripled their investment dollars.

As Mark Twain said, "Few things are harder to put up with than the annoyance of a good example." Well, cringe no more. You can get into real estate in ways you may not have thought possible—and beat those annoying examples at their own game. Let's begin at the beginning—with the roof over your head. Let's buy a house!

Think of how often you've heard someone—maybe even yourself—say, "If only I'd bought back then." Well, then is now! Despite fluctuations in the short-term market, buying a house is still one of the best long-term investments. And, if you get cold feet along the way (as just about everyone does!), keep in mind that the median price for an existing single-family home increased from $38,100 in 1976 to $80,300 in 1986!

To be successful in real estate you must be prepared to act quickly. You have to know when you've got a bargain, when you've found what you want. Perpetual lookers and shoppers never make money in property—they're always waiting for something "just a little bit better" to come along.

Yet in order to move at the right time—whether you're buying a house, a condo, or a chicken farm—you need to be armed with information. The three preparatory steps that follow will enable you to know a good thing when you see it, and to act with confidence.

1) Determine your housing goal and exactly what you can afford well in advance. Decide what the most is that you can pay. Are you seeking shelter, a pure investment, or a combination of the two? Where do you want to be? Are you willing to undertake major repairs or renovations? Are you committed to a certain size house, or are you willing to be flexible? Do you want to do some of the work yourself?

2) Focus on a neighborhood. Once you've selected a town or neighborhood, study it thoroughly. Be prepared to search seriously and to devote time to the hunt. Looking for a house in too wide a geographical area merely results in frustration and confusion. Be ready to look at every house within your price range, as well as those costing a little more. Be flexible about the style and age of the homes you look at.

3) Do your financial homework in advance. Know exactly where you can get a mortgage and at what rate. Develop a working relationship with a banker. Study the bank terms available. Line up an alternative or supplementary loan if you need to. Don't ever wait until you see the house you want to start mortgage shopping. Talk to lenders ahead of time so you'll have an idea of what kind of mortgage you can get and at what terms.

Selecting a House

Location, location, location—these are the three most important elements in buying a home. In the long run it pays to purchase in the best neighborhood you can afford. Your house will appreciate in value faster, and resale will be far easier if your location is a desirable one. And remember, it's almost always better to buy a slightly run-down house in a great area than the best house in a more modest or poorly maintained neighborhood.

Rising property values are fueled by commercial development, good schools, a growing job base, public transportation, and even appealing scenery, such as a beautiful view or a waterfront location. You can also find up-and-coming neighborhoods by talking to brokers who specialize in relocating corporate executives. They know the best areas early on. If properties are selling fast, that too is an indication of a good neighborhood. Ask your broker how long houses remain on the market, and if selling prices are close to asking prices. If the best neighborhood is simply out of your price range, then begin looking in the adjacent towns. Once an area is regarded as chic, smart investors benefit from the "spillover" effect by buying right next door.

Price is something all buyers must determine for themselves. How much mortgage you can afford to carry is based on the amount of your down payment, the type of mortgage you get, and the interest rate. Don't give up too quickly if you think you just can't afford anything; today's creative financing makes it possible for nearly everyone to buy shelter. (Shared equity, buying with a friend, low interest loans, and a myriad of other creative financing methods for the first-time buyer are described in detail in Chapter 24.)

If you're good at carpentry, and are willing to pick up a paint-brush and get your hands dirty, you can save considerably by buying a "fixer-upper." In general these houses cost about 15 percent less than new ones of comparable size, and if you buy a particularly shabby one, your purchase price may be as much as 30 percent less. Fixing the plumbing or screening in the porch yourself often costs *less than half* of what you would pay someone else, and even if you *do* hire a professional, you'll still probably spend less overall than if you'd bought a new house in good condition. Besides, you then have the added advantages of tailoring the house to suit your special needs, and scheduling improvements as you can afford them rather than paying for them in one lump sum.

When looking at property to spruce up, *always* hire a professional house inspector to tell you just how serious the problems are. Go through the entire property with him; ask questions, take notes, and get a written report. You want to know about any major flaws in the foundation, roof, frame, septic system, and the plumbing, wiring, and heating systems. An experienced inspector should also be able to give you a rough estimate of the cost of repairs.

AFFORDABILITY OF A HOUSE

Interest Rate	Monthly Principal and Interest	Property Taxes and Insurance	Total Monthly Expenses	Approx. Annual Income Needed*
9%	$ 724	$200	$ 924	$39,600
11	857	200	1057	45,300
13	996	200	1196	51,257
15	1138	200	1338	57,343
17	1283	200	1483	63,557

Figures based on a 30-year fixed-rate mortgage of $90,000 ($100,000 purchase), with a 10-percent down payment.

*Income requirements may vary, based on other financial obligations.

Buying Below Market Price

More often than not, when you find a house you like it's just a bit over your budget, especially when you factor in closing costs. This calls for clever negotiations on your part, so you can buy below the market or asking price.

There are lots of ways to do this. As you begin your house hunt, continually review the baker's dozen below. Employing even one of them could save you thousands of dollars:

1) Spread the word to everyone you know that you're looking for a house—networking can really pay off.

2) Remember that over 25 percent of all buyers and sellers do not use a broker, so look in the newspapers for owner ads, and don't forget to check local and neighborhood papers—ads there may not appear in city editions.

3) Employ the services of a reliable broker.

4) Look for a seller who *must* move—someone who has been transferred or who is getting divorced is seldom in a position to strike a hard bargain.

5) Look at foreclosed property (see Chapter 5), and at auction and estate sales. Heirs are often anxious to sell, especially if they live far away. Frequently you can buy furniture at the same time.

6) Don't overlook rental homes; owners who live out of town may be renting merely because they could not sell. You may be able to rent with an option to buy.

7) Properties that remain on the market close to a year are often negotiable. Check the tax assessor's office for an up-to-date list of absentee owners.

8) Don't buy the minute a house comes on the market; doing so is an emotional response, and may *not* be a sound business decision.

9) Keep your feelings in rein. If you fall in love with a house (and many people do), try your best not to show it.

10) Occasionally a builder or owner runs out of money, or there's a death in the family, a divorce, or a job transfer. The unfinished home that results can be a risky investment—but can also be a terrific bargain. Investigate the title to make sure there are no liens against it from workmen, and then carefully calculate completion costs. Add at least 30 percent to the estimates given by the construction people, just to be on the safe side. (Workmen commonly underestimate these expenses.)

11) Problem houses are worth considering. Someone else's white elephant could become your shining castle if you are able to come up with creative solutions. Arrange an option to buy while you dream up solutions with your brother-in-law or friend, the handyman.

12) The traditional "handyman special" has made many investors rich. Look beyond dirt and grime and yuk. Visualize fresh paint, wallpaper, new tile, and a freshly mowed lawn. Then add at least 30 percent to the contractor's estimate for repairs and fix-up. Always make a low bid on any home in need of renovation.

13) And, finally, don't lose sight of the fact that the broker works for the seller, *not* for you!

Once you have found the property you like, you must negotiate carefully to keep the price within your range. Follow these hints:

- Keep your emotions to yourself. Once expressed they'll wipe out all your bargaining leverage.

- Think in terms of a "selling price," not the "asking price." Most first-time buyers are unaware of how low a seller may be willing to go. *Bid low.* You can always go higher—and there's always another house.

- Never make an offer without an outside engineer's inspection. Every house has flaws; use them to negotiate. Supplement the engineer's report with your own list of what's wrong.

- Check the county records to find out what the seller paid when he bought the house. Make your offer knowing the seller will probably hold out for some profit.

- Give the owner a limited period (two to three days) to accept your offer. Extra time provides him with the opportunity to check around and be told he can do better. You can say you're considering another property and you don't want to lose it if he's not interested in your offer.

- Beef up a low offer with a sizable "earnest" money deposit. Actual cash on the spot is always enticing. (This check should be made out to an escrow or a trust account.)

2 Co-ops and Condos

The unique thing about cooperatives and condominiums is that they combine the best of two real estate worlds: the financial and fun benefits of ownership, and the simplicity and ease of living in an apartment or townhouse. Some co-ops and condos come with absolutely everything: doormen, maintenance staff, swimming pool, golf, gardens, lawns, elevators, laundry areas, game rooms, and even tennis courts. Add to all this the traditional tax breaks associated with ownership plus appreciation and equity buildup—and you have a winning combination.

There are, of course, trade-offs for having someone else shovel the walks, mow the lawn, and repair the leaks: Not only must you pay extra for these services, you must live in close proximity with other people, sometimes several hundred of them. For many Americans, however (retirees and singles, for instance), this is a great advantage. They enjoy having built-in friends and social activities. For families with small children, community-style living also works well. There are other children to play with, shared babysitting is available, and local schools tend to be good. Security in general is excellent in both co-ops and condos, and the fact that exterior maintenance is taken care of appeals to older people, singles, and working couples.

Before you race out and plunk down your money, let's first distinguish between co-ops and condos. Initially, they may appear to be similar (and in many ways they are); yet there are major differences that affect both your lifestyle and your finances.

Co-ops and condos can be apartment buildings, villas, garden apartments, or townhouses. The key difference between them is type of ownership: A condo owner actually owns his or her unit plus a proportional interest in all the common areas. Alternatively, a co-op owner owns shares in a corporation that in turn owns the entire building; he has a lease to use his individual space.

Condos

In a condo, each owner owns his or her unit directly. Then, together with the other neighbors, he has proportional ownership of the common areas: laundry rooms, storage areas, swimming pools, central air conditioning, hallways, and elevators. The proportion is based on the ratio between the size of the individual unit and the whole complex. If, for example, you own one unit in a 30-unit condo where all units are the same size, your ownership of the common areas is 1/30.

Financing Condos. Because condo owners actually own the units they live in, they must obtain their own mortgages. This is one distinct advantage condos have over co-ops, in which a "blanket" mortgage covers the entire building: personal financing is more difficult to obtain for a co-op, as explained below.

Be sure to check how much monthly maintenance costs are; you'll have to carry these in addition to mortgage payments. These fees cover the cost of ongoing care of the condominium, including maintenance and care of facilities, and a reserve fund for capital repairs. It's interesting to note that unlike co-ops, taxation of common areas in condos is *not* included in monthly maintenance costs. Rather, in almost all cases it is worked into each individual's unit tax assessment.

Renting Your Condo. Condos also make excellent rentals, especially since management firms can take care of the renting process for absentee owners. In fact, nearly one in five condos is owned solely for renting out by investors like yourself. But before you buy a condo with renting in mind, be sure to check the condo rules. Many have restrictions on leasing. Condos often require less involvement with upkeep than single-family homes, since condominium association commonly assumes responsibility for repairs and upkeep; an advantage when renting. And there are tax breaks if you rent out your condo: You can deduct your monthly maintenance payments and depreciation in addition to any mortgage interest and real estate taxes you pay.

Selling Your Condo. You may not always have complete say-so when it comes to selling your condo. The board of directors often has what is called the "right of first refusal." This means you must offer your unit to the board first—for, say, 30 days—to decide if it wants to purchase the unit itself or if it prefers to come up with a purchaser.

If the board fails to do either, you are free to sell to an outsider. These rules vary widely from one condo to another. (Condos almost *always* provide a more flexible arrangement than co-ops, however, where the board *must* approve the purchaser.) You should know what they are, however, before you buy—and before you sell.

Co-ops

A co-op is really a non-profit or limited profit organization that owns the entire building and issues shares of stock to those who live there. Each shareholder has the right to occupy his or her apartment through means of a proprietary lease. Those who live in larger apartments own more shares in the cooperative and pay a higher monthly maintenance. Co-ops are more prevalent in eastern cities, although they exist elsewhere, too. The majority of co-ops are older buildings—the first one appeared on the scene in New York City in the 1880s—and therefore most have already paid off their mortgages. (This by no means makes these co-ops less expensive, however; older buildings tend to incur hefty renovation and repair costs.) Newer co-ops, of course, often have mortgages, and some older ones may have refinanced and so also are mortgaged.

The fact that co-ops are non-profit means they must adhere to the IRS's 80/20 rule: The co-op must obtain at least 80 percent of its income from the shareholders. If the co-op generates more than 20 percent of its income from sources other than the shareholders, the shareholders could conceivably lose their tax deductions.

Financing Co-ops. Bank loans are often more difficult to obtain for co-ops than for condos, primarily because co-op owners are shareholders and not title owners. This means a lender does not have tangible property to be used for collateral. Some banks, however, will allow you to pledge your shares of stock, but generally the terms are difficult and frequently totally unacceptable to the co-op boards. If indeed you are able to get such a mortgage, it will probably be for only about 60 percent of the purchase price, and interest rates may be slightly higher than on a single-family house. The co-op board may also limit or completely disallow borrowing using co-op shares as collateral. Because of these inherent difficulties, co-op buyers have traditionally financed their apartments through personal loans.

However, starting in 1984, mortgage lenders have been able to offer co-op mortgages through the Federal National Mortgage Association (Fannie Mae) program. Since then other lending institutions have eased up on their policies for granting mortgages. Ask your local bank what type of financing is available.

The Issue of Monthly Assessments. When a co-op has a mortgage, it is called a "blanket" mortgage, since it covers the entire building. Stockholders are assessed each month for their pro-rata share of this mortgage, of taxes, and of maintenance. These assessments are lumped into one "monthly maintenance" payment, which also covers maintenance, care of private roads and recreational facilities, garbage pick-up, snow removal, lawn care, and the like. In a co-op, these fees include mortgage and tax payments, whereas in a condo they do not. Be prepared, too, for special assessments for repairs and other emergencies.

More often than not, monthly assessments in both condos and co-ops turn out to be greater than you anticipated, or they may increase faster than you'd like. But you must pay them. Failure to do so could lead to a lien against your property, and eventually your unit could be sold to pay off the debt.

Selling Your Co-op. In a co-op, the stockholders have a direct concern regarding the creditworthiness of all other owners—and for good reason: If one defaults and cannot pay his maintenance and share of the building's mortgage, the other stockholders may ultimately be responsible for that share. And, when it's time for you to sell, the co-op board may be tough; it might exercise its right of first refusal and reject a prospective buyer it does not feel is creditworthy. (The board may not reject a buyer for purposes of racial, sexual, or religious discrimination.)

Although co-op boards usually reject potential buyers for financial reasons, they have also been known to turn down rock stars or other public figures in order to maintain privacy and quiet.

Governing Boards

Living in either a co-op or a condo entails becoming a member of a small village, governed by an elected board of directors. When you buy your property or your shares, you automatically become a member of the board association or council. Your voting rights are usually determined by the size or value of your unit in relation to that of the whole building or complex. You may either vote or assign your votes by proxy at the annual or monthly meetings. However, it is important

to keep in touch with what your association and board are doing—
you have a large investment in your co-op or condo, and decisions
made by the directors will directly affect your life and the value of
your real estate.

Before you buy in, read your co-op or condo's bylaws. Among the
items covered are: nominations of board members and the election
process, the building's budget, architectural details, rental of units,
sale and financing procedures, and restrictions regarding such things
as children, pets, or operating a business from the building. Be
certain to read any clauses pertaining to the board's right to first
refusal on a unit's sale. As discussed above, this will affect you
directly when and if you decide to sell.

The Interview

Once you have selected a co-op or a condo, there will be one last step
to take before you can actually make a purchase. In a co-op you *must*
be okayed by the board of directors, and in some condos an interview
may also be required. Board members may question you on a variety
of things, and it's best to be well prepared.

Before the interview:

- Ask your real estate broker what the board members are like.

- Dress appropriately. Do not be too casually attired.

- Ask what documents you should bring.

- Make a list of business and personal references.

- Make a list of questions to ask the board of directors.

At the interview:

- Be prepared to answer questions about your finances, your work
  experience, and probably on your personal life.

- If you are paying for the apartment with a large loan from a
  relative or bank, the board will want to know about your ability
  to make the monthly maintenance fees in addition to large
  mortgage payments.

- You may be asked to disclose your income tax returns and explain
  any noticeable variations in income. Self-employed people and

free-lancers, in particular, are queried about their often mercurial income stream.

- Don't be afraid to ask questions of the committee. Speak up. Participate, but don't grill them in a critical tone.

- Use this interview to find out about the co-op or condo as well as to let the board find out about you.

3 Manufactured Homes

The least expensive quality shelter available today is a manufactured home, and yet most investors overlook this form of housing. Prices are low, quality is high, and financing plentiful.

Manufactured homes were once called mobile homes, because even those mobile homes that were permanently installed were moved to their site as a whole house (unlike "prefabs," which come in sectional units). But since these homes are permanent residences — their wheels and axles are not for continuous use — they are no longer referred to as mobile homes. The U.S. Congress recognized this fact in 1980, when it changed the name to "manufactured homes" on all official documents and in the federal laws.

The average new manufactured home costs only $21,800 and includes two bedrooms, one bath, all appliances, *and* furniture. And within the manufactured home category there are plenty of homes priced for less — $8,400 for a new single-width home (12 to 14 feet wide, and 48 to 76 feet long) — and for more — $30,100 for a luxury double-width model (24 to 28 feet wide, and 36 to 76 feet long). There are 140 companies that build manufactured homes throughout the country; homes generally range from 400 to 2,500 square feet. The "Florida special," a 12-foot-wide, one-bedroom home with less than 500 square feet of space, costs only $6,900 and is suitable for living in four to six months a year.

Second-hand manufactured homes are also available. Older single-width models can often be purchased for very little money, especially if they are already in a manufactured home park. Check the classified real estate section in your newspaper, or your local yellow pages, and call dealers and parks for leads.

In addition to the purchase price of your home, you will have to pay approximately $3,000 for delivery and installation. And, unless you own land, you will have to pay monthly rent to the owner of a manufactured home park. Rents vary widely depending upon location and the amenities offered. In Florida, for example, they range from $60 per month for the simplest space to $350 for an all-adult community with a golf course and swimming.

In 1976, federal law mandated that all manufactured homes meet the same minimum safety and building standards, and the results have been impressive: Manufactured homes are now regarded twice as safe in terms of fire than all other types of housing. This makes them easier to insure and finance.

Financing

Manufactured homes qualify for all types of loans as long as they are permanently installed. The most common is a retail installment contract, arranged directly through the retailer or by the homebuyer with a financial institution.

The Veterans Administration (VA) guarantees loans for the purchase of both new and existing homes for up to 50 percent of the principal amount or $20,000, whichever is less. No down payment is required under the VA loan program; however, one may be required by the lending institution granting the loan.

FHA Loans. The FHA provides that federal insurance be given to financial institutions for loans covering the purchase of a manufactured home. Guidelines are the same as for mortgages on regular single-family homes (see Chapter 24). Mortgages are insured for up to 30 years, and the down payment is generally three to five percent, unless the lending institution requires more. The maximum allowable mortgage varies from state to state, so check your local office regarding current regulations.

Location

If you own land then you're all set, although you should be certain to check the local zoning laws before ordering a manufactured home for delivery. But if you are not a landowner, you would be unwise to buy a home until you have a spot to put it in.

Manufactured Home Communities

There are 24,000 traditional rental communities nationwide, encompassing 1.8 million homesites. New communities average 150 to 175 sites each, and rentals range from $50 to $300 per month, with the majority falling between $80 and $150.

Begin your search for a site by investigating nearby communities regarding space. In many cases there's a long waiting list. Take time to visit several communities, and talk to management as well as to residents. Among the points to consider are:

- How often and by how much are rents raised?

- What fees are there?

- Are pets or children permitted?

- Are there any rules about guests?

- How much does fuel cost?

- Is there a tenants' group?

- Under what circumstances can one be evicted?

While it is still popular to buy a manufactured home and then rent a homesite with utilities, an increasing number of homeowners are buying their own land, often in cooperatively-owned developments. Lenders are starting to provide mortgage financing for these community sites. For example, the Federal Housing Administration (FHA) will insure loans on new manufactured home rental development communities and for existing communities that are going through rehabilitation. The FHA currently guarantees loans for up to 90 percent of the appraised value of the site. The per-site limitation is $9,000, with up to a 75-percent increase permitted in high-cost areas.

Note: According to the National Association of Manufactured Homes, these homes appreciate just like other forms of housing *as long as* they are permanently installed and have some type of structure added on, such as a carport, sunporch, patio, greenhouse, etc. The higher the quality of the land-lease community in which the home is placed, the greater the appreciation. If your own piece of property is well located, appreciation will be all the more rapid and impressive.

BECOME AN EXPERT

Further information is provided in the following publications:

- *Manufactured Home News*
  $25/year
  Gidder House Publishing
  706 Tunn Bull Road
  Altamonte Springs, FL 32715
  305-830-7300

- *MobileHome Parks Report*
  $125/year
  Parks Publishing Co.
  4412 The Court
  Sacramento, CA 95821
  916-971-0489

For consumer complaints that cannot be resolved with the manufacturer, contact:

- Manufactured Housing: Program Compliance
  U.S. Housing & Urban Development Department
  451 Seventh Street, S.W.
  Washington, D.C. 20410
  202-755-7184

For a copy of *How to Buy a Manufactured Home*, a 24-page booklet which covers warranty, site preparation, and installation, send 50 cents and a large, self-addressed envelope to:

- Consumer Information Center
  P.O. Box 453
  Pueblo, CO 81009

For a copy of *Quick Facts About the Manufactured Housing Industry*, write to:

- Manufactured Housing Institute
  1745 Jefferson Davis Highway
  Arlington, VA 22202
  703-979-6620

4 Buying Abroad

A country house in England, a studio in Paris, or a condo on the coast of Spain. Fantasies? Not anymore. Buying property abroad makes economic sense for those who travel extensively, who have family in other countries, who want a retirement home, or who want to vacation part time and earn rental income the rest of the year. You may also make money if your property appreciates and you can sell at a profit, or if your purchase and sale take advantage of the difference in value between the dollar and the currency of the country in which you buy.

In selecting a foreign property you must investigate the situation even more thoroughly than you would if you were buying domestically. But if you purchase at the right time and price, you can reap economic benefits by renting—and eventually selling, if you so choose. In fact, there may be *better* real estate opportunities abroad than in the U.S.—even for the first-time investor—depending on the strength of the dollar and other factors detailed below. Among the points to keep in mind are:

- **Currency.** What is the value of the dollar *vis à vis* the foreign currency? Check the financial pages of the newspaper and try to time your purchase to take advantage of the exchange rate.

- **Risks.** Invest only in countries with stable governments. You certainly don't want your holdings confiscated or their value to drop sharply due to political fluctuations.

- **Convenience.** If this is important to you, buy in an area near major airports. This is also a factor in renting.

- **Renting.** If you plan to rent your chalet or castle when you're not in residence, make certain someone else can handle the details for you. Condos or villas in well-managed resort areas are easier to rent than isolated homes (although the right wealthy person

19

might be willing to pay for a secluded summer retreat.

- **Finances.** It is generally difficult to arrange financing through foreign banks. Few ever grant mortgages to non-citizens. However, sometimes new resorts or large complexes will offer some financing. Your three most likely sources are: 1) remortgaging your property in the U.S.; 2) a possible mortgage from a U.S. bank with offices in the foreign country in which you are buying; and 3) a loan from the seller. Keep in mind that cash payment may give you a 10- to 20-percent discount on the price.

- **Taxes.** Consult with a knowledgeable accountant about the foreign country's taxation policy on rental income and proceeds should you sell your property. There are also specific U.S. tax rules regarding ownership of foreign property. Tax regulations are ever-changing, so it's important to be up to date. You could be subject to dual taxation.

Finding Property Abroad

If you have friends who have purchased abroad, begin your hunt with their help. In addition, you should read the real estate ads in the leading international newspapers, such as the Sunday *New York Times*, the *Wall Street Journal*, the *International Herald Tribune*, and the *London Times*, as well as in the major papers in the city of your choice.

BECOME AN EXPERT

Several U.S. firms maintain up-to-date property listings:

- Previews, Inc.
  New York, NY
  212-557-4466

- Begg International
  Washington, D.C.
  202-387-2480

- Sotheby's International Realty
  New York, NY
  212-606-7660

Also available in bookstores and libraries:

- *Tax and Trade Guides* (published by Arthur Anderson, they cover the major countries)

- *Doing Business* (published by Price, Waterhouse, this series covers a number of foreign places)

- *Country Studies Handbook* (published by American University)

5 Buying at Auction

If you know your facts, have patience, and are a little bit lucky, you can buy real estate at "fire-sale" prices at an auction. When a property owner defaults on his mortgage payments, it may be sold at a public auction to pay this debt. Anyone may bid on publicly-auctioned real estate. Often, those who sell at auction must get rid of property in a hurry, and they're not apt to hold out for the best price.

Last year, lenders, banks and government agencies, including the Veterans Administration and the Department of Housing & Urban Development (HUD), repossessed approximately 100,000 houses and condos across the country. Some of this real estate was repossessed from people who were unable to meet their mortgage payments; some was from developers in a financial squeeze. Banks, lien holders (see Chapter 22), and financially troubled builders who need to unload properties enable investors/buyers to find values 5 to 25 percent below the going price.

Perhaps you feel it would be difficult to benefit from someone else's troubles. But remember that in the majority of cases, these foreclosed homes have already been vacant for some time, having been auctioned off at what is usually known as a sheriff's sale. (Buying at this auction is not advisable since many states grant a buy-back period of from six months to a year, during which the previous owner may buy back his or her house for the amount due on the mortgage. Generally, the only buyers at a sheriff's auction are lenders who want to get clear title to the property they financed, so they can turn around and sell it again—perhaps to you!)

Types of Auctions

After lenders get a free and clear title, they can do one of three things: 1) hold their own public auction; 2) negotiate a sale directly with individual buyers; or 3) deal with a real estate agent. This is the point at which it is advantageous for you to enter into the proceedings, because the bank or lender wants to unload the property as soon as possible to avoid upkeep costs. Prices, therefore, are low.

There are three different types of auction. You should know their distinctive features prior to bidding on property.

- **An absolute auction.** The highest bidder wins, and the seller cannot renege or make any changes.

- **An auction with reservations.** The seller retains the right to reject the highest bid within a stated time period. This is often the case with corporation and estate sales where approval must be obtained from a board of directors or from heirs.

- **An auction subject to upset price.** An advertised minimum is set prior to the bidding. The property cannot be sold for less.

How to Find Auction Property

Read your local paper or newsletters specializing in listing such properties for auction dates and locations. Auctioneers also maintain lists of properties to be sold. Or, call the real estate department of local banks for their lists. If you are willing to take an unwanted house off the bank's hands, it is frequently willing to negotiate better mortgage rates for you, perhaps foregoing or reducing points. (Points are commonly charged by lending institutions when a mortgage is processed; one point is equal to one percent of the amount of the mortgage.) In some cases, you can acquire such property for very little or no money down. In addition, the bank may assume some of the closing costs.

The unloading of real estate owned properties (REOs) by banks and other lenders has created a network of services that match sellers and buyers. One of the largest is the R.E.O. Institute, Inc., located in Beverly Hills. It lists distressed single-family condos, duplexes, apartment buildings, and even small businesses. Similar services are available in most metropolitan areas. Ask your bank or real estate broker for names.

You'll have to make certain preparations before you bid at an auction. Be sure to visit the property you're interested in, preferably with an engineer or inspector. You'll also want a professional appraisal, to help determine the top price you'd be willing to pay.

Come to the auction with a certified check to cover your initial deposit. The amount required is generally stated in the advertisement; be prepared with $2,000 to $5,000. (Deposits usually are not refundable, so don't bid unless you qualify for financing.) Finally, keep your cool; don't overbid; there will always be another auction.

After the auction, you will have only about 45 days to obtain financing. Your best bet, then, is probably to approach the lending institution that is auctioning off the property, especially if it is essentially a sound investment and the owner was unable to meet the mortgage payments. Do this as far in advance of the auction as possible, to allow maximum time for financing to come through.

Many of the nation's reputable auctioneers ask real estate brokers to attend their sales. You can arrange for one of these brokers to act on your behalf. They will register your name with the auctioneer. Then, if the bid placed for you by the broker wins, the auctioneer and the broker will share the commission.

Federal Housing Administration Foreclosures

Keep in mind that the Federal Housing Administration and the Veterans Administration also sell distressed property, usually through real estate brokers. Most of these houses are small and modestly priced to begin with—generally from $35,000 to $55,000— although many require extensive repairs. The Department of Housing and Urban Development (HUD) lists those available on a weekly basis. Ask your local HUD office or area broker for a copy, or call HUD in Washington, D.C., at 202-775-6422.

For a free copy of "How To Buy a Foreclosed Home," write to:

- REO Consumer Brochure
  P.O. Box 23867
  Baltimore, MD 21203

For a list of foreclosed homes for sale, contact:

- Federal National Mortgage Association (Fannie Mae)
  3900 Wisconsin Avenue, N.W.
  Washington, D.C. 20016
  202-537-7000

For information on "The REO Registry" ($150 for three months), which lists over 1,000 foreclosed properties for sale every month, write to:

- The REO Institute
  P.O. Box 5504
  Beverly Hills, CA 90210

Buying City-Owned Property

Municipal real estate is also available by auction, often at reasonable prices. Advertisements for city auctions appear in local newspapers.

Municipal real estate becomes available through tax forfeitures, mortgage foreclosures, abandonment of property, and excess highway land. Rules and procedures vary within each bureaucracy, and you must count on miles of red tape. The basic facts, though, are similar:

- Public auctions are held once or twice a year.

- Ads appear in the local newspapers.

- Municipal, state, and federal housing agencies maintain mailing lists announcing forthcoming auctions.

- Detailed brochures or listing sheets are provided for each piece of property. They tell the stated minimum bid, the size of the property, its appraised value, payment procedures, and pertinent building codes.

- 10 percent of the appraised minimum bid is usually required as a down payment; it must be made with a cashier's check.

Financing terms are often surprisingly flexible: For example, at a San Diego auction of city property, buyers were required to pay 10 percent down and then had an option of either paying the entire purchase price within 30 days, or paying 30 percent within the month and then making quarterly payments (including interest) over a five-year period.

Houses for a Dollar

The Urban Homestead Program, created under the Housing and Community Development Act of 1974, transfers federally-owned unoccupied houses to state and local agencies, which then sell them for only one dollar. These homestead houses are all foreclosed properties that were FHA, VA, or Farmers Home Mortgage financed. After foreclosure they go into what's called a federal inventory for 30 days. The Department of Housing and Urban Development (HUD) decides to take over some of these foreclosed houses, which are then made available to the people in the area. HUD solicits applications from low- to moderate-income families, and since there are so many, they hold a lottery or in some areas decide who should get the homes via committee. (The houses that HUD does not take are then turned over to local realtors who have signed a non-discriminatory statement. The public can then buy them through these real estate brokers.) The purpose of the program is to put these houses back on the city's tax rolls and at the same time help moderately low-income families find shelter.

Qualifications for being a homesteader and the screening process are determined at the local level. However, according to the national office, most homesteaders have incomes between 65 and 85 percent of the median income in their area. If homesteaders earn below the 65-

percent benchmark, they are likely to have difficulty paying rehabilitation loans (as explained below). Because there are more hopeful homesteaders than available properties, and because these houses are such a good bargain, most cities and towns use a lottery system to assign houses. Chicago, for example, where income requirements range between $20,500 and $36,000 (depending upon the size of the family), holds a lottery every other year.

Nearly all homestead properties require rehabilitation to bring them up to official building code standards. Participating lending institutions provide loans at rates as low as three percent for this purpose. Most programs require the new owners to live in the homestead for a minimum of five years.

BECOME AN EXPERT

For more information contact your regional HUD office, or send for a copy of "Urban Homesteading":

- U.S. Dept. of Housing & Urban Development
  451 7th Street, S.W.
  Washington, D.C. 20410
  202-453-4527

The classic means of making money has always been to sell something for a profit, whether it's 100 shares of IBM or 100 acres of lakefront property. But if selling the dream house you worked so long and hard to buy is the last thing you can imagine doing, you may wonder if you'll ever reap the benefits of your investment.

There is one way to generate a profit and still own your property—and that's by becoming a landlord. You can begin small, by renting out a spare bedroom or an empty garage space. And then, if you like being a part-time landlord and if you enjoy dealing with people, it's fairly simple to move into the big time—to run a Bed & Breakfast inn or perhaps even invest in rentable commercial space. Or, for something completely different, you could rent your home to a filmmaker who wants to use your living room or the pool in your back yard in his next movie or TV commercial.

And no matter who becomes your tenant—a stranger or a relative—if you follow the guidelines outlined here you can also benefit from a number of special tax breaks for landlords.

6 Renting Out a Room

The least expensive and at the same time the easiest way to become involved in real estate may be one you've never considered, and yet it's right under your own roof—taking in a boarder. Rent provided by a tenant will immediately help with the mortgage and taxes, give you extra income on a regular basis, and provide a little companionship if you're all alone. Housemates often share utility bills and other maintenance costs, too.

You may want to consider taking in a boarder for several different reasons: if your children have left home and you have a spare room, if you're divorced and need some extra income, or just for fun.

Renting out a room will, of course, change your life to some extent—you will suddenly be responsible for someone else's living comfort and you'll also be giving up a certain degree of privacy. On the other hand, a tenant can provide welcome companionship and security for the lonely and elderly. But before you hang out a ROOM FOR RENT sign, check your local zoning laws to make certain your area permits such arrangements.

How much you'll be able to charge depends upon the facilities you can offer. Obviously, if your boarder has his or her own bath, you will be able to command a higher price than if these facilities are shared. If the space is on a floor or in a wing separate from yours, you can also ask for more. For pricing guidelines, check with one or two local realtors and with others who have rented out rooms.

Always ask for at least two months' rent in advance, the first for the first month's rent, and the last to ensure receiving 30 days' notice prior to a tenant's leaving. A security deposit, up to 75 percent of one month's rent, is also recommended.

Also, keep in mind that there are a number of expenses you'll probably incur for such things as extra insurance, lawyer's or realtor's fees, bedroom furniture, curtains, linens, towels, rugs, etc.

You should have a written agreement, preferably one checked or drawn up by a lawyer. Among the specifics to include are:

- The amount of the security deposit (and terms of return of the deposit)

- How utilities are to be divided (if the boarder pays a fixed percentage, you won't be forced to raise the rent if these costs rise)

- Who will pay for repairs and maintenance, and to what extent

- Whether pets, guests, smoking, and cooking are allowed

- Rules pertaining to noise and late hours

- Procedures for entering and exiting (you may want your renter to use a side door or back staircase, especially early in the morning or late at night)

- Parking

You can obtain copies of sample contracts from a real estate broker or a stationer. Compare them to see how they are drawn up and what the different arrangements are for who pays for what.

Before actually taking in a boarder, review your insurance policy. You want to be properly covered. Boarders should carry their own tenant's insurance to cover all personal possessions.

SAMPLE RENTS FOR SINGLE ROOMS

Boston, MA	$80 to $90 per week
Chicago, IL	$80 to $95 per week
Los Angeles, CA	$40 to $65 per week
Miami, FL	$80 to $90 per week
New York, NY	$85 to $100 per week
St. Louis, MO	$65 to $85 per week
St. Petersburg, FL	$60 to $70 per week
Silver Springs, MD	$75 to $85 per week
Washington, DC	$90 to $100 per week

(Compiled by E.F. Research Associates)

Tax Advantages

A number of the costs involved in being a landlord may be tax deductible, but often only up to the limit of your rental income. You are allowed a pro-rata share of such expenses as heat, light, insurance, mortgage interest, real estate taxes, and the cost of advertising. A part of the upkeep and a percentage of depreciation are also deductible. The exact amounts will depend on the number of rooms you rent, their size in relation to your entire house, and the age of your house. Your accountant can help you determine these dollar amounts.

If your house is treated as an income-producing property you must be aware of the over-age-55 guidelines: If you have rented for five years prior to selling your house and you are 55 or older when you sell, you could lose the one-time capital gains tax exclusion of up to $125,000. But if you do not rent three out of the five years prior to the sale, you will still qualify for the $125,000 exclusion.

If you need someone to help you out—either to care for young children, an elderly parent, or a disabled family member—you may be able to work out a special arrangement with your boarder, reducing the rent in exchange for a certain number of hours of assistance per week or per month. You should check with your accountant, however, about the possible tax impact of such an arrangement.

Tax Consequences

If at some point you decide to sell your home, you *must* pay a capital gains tax on the sale proceeds for that portion of the home that was rented out, regardless of whether or not you then purchase another home. (When no rental situation is involved, you do not have to pay capital gains on the sale of a home if you purchase another home of equal or greater value.)

BECOME AN EXPERT

For further information get a copy of the IRS booklet #527, entitled "Rental Property," from the Forms Distribution Center nearest you:

- P.O. Box 25866
  Richmond, VA 23268

- P.O. Box 12626
  Fresno, CA 93778

- P.O. Box 9903
  Bloomington, IL 61799

- P.O. Box 408
  Church St. Station
  New York, NY 10008

7 Renting Out Your Home

Although you may aspire to become a real estate magnate with luxurious properties stretching across the nation, it's easiest to begin in your own backyard—by renting out a single-family house. Later on, after making your initial profit, you can add to your holdings and eventually move into commercial real estate (see Chapter 8). By then, what began as a hobby may have turned into a full-time career.

If you're concerned about getting started, consider the facts already at your fingertips: 1) You know the neighborhoods in the area—the desirable and the not-so-desirable; 2) you know the best school districts; 3) you can learn through the grapevine who is moving; 4) you know the reliable real estate brokers; 5) you've already worked with tradesmen and helpers; and 6) you're familiar with banks in the vicinity.

Yet, before you begin your hunt, consider what it means to be a landlord.

The Landlord's Role

Pipes break, furnaces go out, grass grows, windows get rattly. Repairs are a constant. So are Sunday morning calls from tenants. So, before you put a For Rent ad in the paper, or before buying rental property, think carefully about all that's involved in being a landlord. If the thought of handling leaky faucets and deadbeat renters is burdensome, then consider using a professional management company, or simply move on to another chapter in this book!

Management companies charge fees which vary greatly depending on where the property is located, its type and size. Plan on 5 to 10 percent of the gross income. If you own a small home or a duplex apartment, a management company hardly makes sense; on the other hand, a large apartment building, or two or three rental houses is more than even the best handyman can take care of all alone.

Residential Property

This is the easiest area for most beginning investors. Not only does it offer the best loans at the lowest rates, but it is also the simplest to rent. Keep in mind, however, that single-family homes require more upkeep and maintenance per rental unit or per tenant than do apartment houses. You can address this situation to some extent through clauses in the lease requiring the tenant to mow the lawn, shovel the snow, and take care of small repairs (although certainly not the furnace, air conditioner, or roof).

It's generally wisest to buy the type of home you yourself would be willing to live in. Houses in poor condition only lead to more problems and consistently attract undesirable tenants. However, if you buy an extremely expensive home, you will be limited as to the number of people who can afford to rent it. (If they have that much money, they'd probably prefer to own, too.) The best category by far is the medium-priced home in a stable neighborhood with a good public school system. The ideal rental is a 3-bedroom, 1½-bath house suitable for a small family and yet easy to sell. You can boost your profit potential by buying houses that need improvement *if* you're good at repairs — or your brother-in-law is.

Here are some important guidelines for investing in single-family rentals:

- Do not buy a house that does not immediately provide a positive monthly cash flow.

- Buy the shabbiest house on a good block.

- Buy a deteriorating house in an improving neighborhood.

- Buy in your own backyard, where you know the trends, the caliber of the schools, the tax base, and the employment possibilities.

- If you already live in town and are buying a second home to rent out, check with neighbors to see who's moving. If you discover a handyman special, buying in your own backyard is to your advantage since you already know a local plumber, electrician, and *his* brother-in-law, the carpenter. You also know the right side of the tracks and the best school districts.

- Buy from someone who needs to sell: a distant heir, someone newly divorced or who is about to undergo a job transfer, or someone who has already purchased another house and must unload his first home quickly.

- Buy an empty house; the owner is probably anxious to sell it.

- Decorate attractively, but on the cheap.

- Hire others to do repair work, too. The IRS does not let you deduct your own labor costs, but salaries paid to workers — including members of your family, if you pay them the market rate — are deductible. (This is exclusive of capital improvements, which are depreciated over 19 years, rather than deducted.)

Determining Rent. The rule of thumb is an annual rent of 9 percent of the market value of your home, but that's not a sure bet. In areas where there are very few vacancies, rents are extremely high. The opposite, of course, is also true — low rents in high vacancy areas. Check your local newspaper and several real estate brokers for dollar suggestions. Ideally, rent should cover all monthly operating expenses, such as mortgage, insurance, maintenance, taxes, and repairs. Negotiate with your tenant, if you have not decided ahead of time, things like who will pay for heat and who will cut the lawn. Whatever arrangement works for both parties is fine as long as it's spelled out in the lease.

ANNUAL EXPENSES BEFORE TAXES

Mortgage payment	$_____
Real estate taxes	_____
Maintenance expenses	_____
Miscellaneous	_____
Total cost of carrying house	$_____

Divide last figure by 12 to determine *minimum* monthly rent you must receive

---

Expenses. In addition to your mortgage payments and taxes, when renting you must also budget for advertising, tenant credit checks, homeowner's insurance, and in some instances a management or broker's fee. If you have several houses to rent, you may wish to hire a professional manager. If so, plan on paying the manager 5 to 10 percent of the annual rent, plus a charge of 50 to 100 percent of one month's rent for locating and screening tenants.

Tenants. Before you advertise or list your house with an agent, decide who you do not want living in your place: dogs, cats, children, smokers, more than a certain number of people. Also, check local laws—particularly in university communities—about the maximum number of unrelated people ("groupers") who may live in one dwelling. Then determine if your prospective tenants can afford the rent. It should be no more than 30 percent of their income. Review references (including salary) very carefully, and if necessary run a credit check. It's also best to meet the tenant in person, if possible, or even to visit him where he currently lives. You'll get a good idea of how he'll take care of your rental property by getting a first-hand look at his present living situation.

If you advertise for tenants, arrange for all those who respond to view the house or apartment within the same two- to three-hour time period. That way you won't waste your time with numerous individual showings. Be wary of applicants who can move in tomorrow—they may have been evicted from their former residence!

It's a smart policy to require your renters to leave a refundable security deposit—a week's or month's rent, depending upon the length of time of the rental. In case there is trouble you can use this deposit to cover your insurance deductible. Include a clause in the lease allowing you to inspect the exterior of the property once a month and the interior once every two months. Also, ask your tenant to give at least two months' notice if he or she is not planning to renew the lease, as well as permission to show the house to new prospective tenants. You may want to offer a reduction in the rent (say $25) for those months when payment is received by the first.

Full-Service Realtor. If you want to invest but have little time to look for suitable rental property, you can use a full-service broker—one who finds the house, packages the financing, manages the rental, and when the time comes, sells it for you. You can sometimes get financing through a full-service broker at or below bank rates with no closing costs. Of course, in return you pay a fee. The primary advantage is obviously not monetary, but the time you save in hunting for property.

Insurance. Before you turn over the key to your tenants, check with the agent who handles your homeowner's insurance to make sure your policy is appropriate for a rental situation. You should also consider increasing your personal liability insurance to protect yourself. A tenant who stumbles down your basement stairs may just decide to sue.

You'll also need to guard against theft if you are renting out a furnished home. If your policy contains a clause similar to "coverage does not include any part of theft or loss when rented to another party or parties," talk to your agent about a so-called "all-risk" policy. It will probably cost 10 to 15 percent more, but if you're renting on a regular basis, it's worth it. Even greater coverage is possible through a more expensive "special multi-peril policy," which even takes care of damaged furniture. You might also suggest to your tenants that they may want renter's insurance to cover their own possessions, too.

Tax Implications

The new tax rulings are complicated and vary widely depending upon income, losses, deductions, other types of investments, and your age. It is *essential* that you discuss each rental situation with your accountant. In general, however, you should know that:

- Depreciation (see Appendix) on residential rental property is 27.5 years. Depreciation is the cost of wear and tear plus age of your property. When you rent out your house, you can deduct the mortgage interest, real estate taxes, repairs, and insurance, *plus* depreciation. But if you live in your house, you can only deduct the mortgage interest and real estate taxes. The 1986 tax law stretched out the depreciation time from 19 to 27.5 years for residential property. You can still write off the same amount, but just over a longer period of time.

- The taxable income (or tax losses, if depreciation and other allowable deductions exceed the amount you receive in rent) on rental property is considered "passive"; this means you cannot use those tax losses to offset your salary or portfolio income unless your gross income is less than $100,000. If it is, you can take up to $25,000 in losses on rental property you actively manage. In order to qualify as "active" you must own 10 percent of the property and personally make decisions about tenants, rents, repairs. If you hire a manager you can still fall under the "active" category if you can prove that you guide such decisions.

- The new law diminishes the benefit of losses if your adjusted gross income is between $100,000 and $150,000. For every $1 in income over $100,000, you lose the ability to currently deduct 50 cents of allowable losses. For example, if you earn $110,000 then you can currently deduct a maximum of only $20,000 (although losses in excess of this amount can be carried forward to offset future passive income).

- If you make more than $150,000, things can change dramatically. Your tax shelter status will be determined by many other factors, including other passive activity holdings, how long you have held them, and whether a profit or loss is realized. Consult your account.

- Depending on your income and other factors, rental homes may enjoy other tax benefits, such as write-offs of real estate taxes, mortgage interest, insurance, travel to and from the property, paint, labor (although not your own), and repairs.

BECOME AN EXPERT

For further information, send for a copy of IRS booklet #527, entitled "Rental Property," from the Forms Distribution center below nearest you.

- P.O. Box 25866
  Richmond, VA 23268

- P.O. Box 12626
  Fresno, CA 93778

- P.O. Box 9903
  Bloomington, IL 61799

- P.O. Box 408
  Church St. Station
  New York, NY 10008

8 | Commercial Real Estate

With time and money you can make a fortune in commercial real estate—just look at Donald Trump or Conrad Hilton! It's definitely not an area for the timid, yet if you begin small—perhaps with a store or a two-family house, and in your own backyard where you know the turf—then you, too, can become a real estate king.

Investing Directly in Commercial Property

Before considering investing in an office building, apartment house, or store, you should be aware of the sobering reality: Commercial real estate is *always* risky despite what any sales person or developer may tell you. It is affected by a myriad of forces, many of which are beyond your control: population shifts, traffic flow, competition, fads, etc.

Because of the enormous risks involved and the large capital required, most individuals with a hankering for commercial property invest instead in REITs and RELPs (see Chapters 16 and 17). Yet, there are always opportunities available for the adventuresome. Here are several ideas to inspire creativity in shopping.

Invest locally. You know the population, traffic patterns, economic level, and real estate prices in your own backyard. Look for a vacant school or bank, an office or small store that can be fixed up, or an old railroad station or building with historic charm. Vacated gas stations can be turned into florist shops, convenience stores, and even restaurants.

If you need an office for your own work, buy or build one, and then use part of it for yourself and rent out the rest.

If the house you already live in is in an area that's going commercial, you can convert it to an office or store and rent out sections of it.

Small rental units are the safest choice for most non-professional investors. Whereas in most parts of the country it is fairly easy to find tenants for apartments, the same is not necessarily true of commercial space. In many areas, office space is currently overbuilt and going begging for tenants. (Houston, Denver, New Orleans, and Ft. Lauderdale have dropped rents by as much as 20 percent since 1982.) If a small shopping center loses several tenants, it could spell disaster. And, of course, it's easier for an individual to buy and supervise an apartment or two than a huge complex.

Find out what the current rents and expenses are — projected figures may be inaccurate. Don't fall for the old line, "When the lease expires you'll be able to double the rent!" Find out if rents are fixed for several years; if so they may not cover increased expenses.

CASH FLOW FOR COMMERCIAL REAL ESTATE

Cash flow is the net profit or loss that results from collecting rental income and paying out expenses, as detailed below[*]:

Current Rental Income:	$36,000
Minus **operating expenses**[**]:	(12,000)
Minus **vacancy reserves (10%):**	(3,600)
Equals:	$20,400
Minus **mortgage and interest payments:**	(18,000)
Equals **cash flow:**	$2,400

[*]Sample assumes rental income of $3,000 per month, $1,500 monthly payment on a $200,000 mortgage, and operating expenses of $1,000 per month.

[**]Expenses include management, real estate taxes, repairs, insurance, and utilities.

Selecting Commercial Real Estate

Although commercial property varies widely from place to place and type to type, there are several guidelines you can use to protect yourself.

Spend time researching. Know land values, building costs, zoning laws, sources of financing, tax regulations, land use stipulations, and the market potential. This information is essential to finding a potentially solid investment and should not be entrusted to anyone else.

Assemble a team of experts. You'll need a real estate lawyer, an accountant familiar with real estate tax laws in your area, and a reputable real estate broker. Money spent for top-notch advisers is well worth it, especially if you're a first-time investor.

Greater profit may lie in building rather than purchasing an existing structure. Starting from scratch can be especially advantageous if you get your land at a good price and keep your building costs low—*and* it will allow you to tailor the building to your particular needs. However, if through repairs and renovation you can boost the value of an existing building noticeably, then by all means, make your fortune that way. Consider all possibilities before you buy.

If you own land, you will need to work with a contractor. If the two of you become partners, then the contractor will do the building and pay half the costs (although you will, of course, have to pay him for his time). The great advantage to this arrangement is that the contractor has a vested interest in the building and is therefore likely to do a first-rate construction job at a reasonable cost.

If you renovate an existing building, check with the local officials regarding zoning ordinances and land-use regulations. These change over the years, so be certain you're up to date. The town hall will also tell you what permits you need. Have a qualified engineer evaluate the physical condition of the building. (The main elements to check for are adequate plumbing and heating, and a sound overall structure.)

You may be able to get the current owner to finance some of the improvements; this will reduce the financial burden weighing on your shoulders.

Always make an offer based on a report by an independent building engineer. This inspection is vital and will unearth any major weaknesses in the building.

Risks Involved

You should be well aware of the potential risks in commercial real estate. This is a cyclical industry that responds primarily to the welfare of the nation or the area's economy. The most crucial problem you may encounter is potential losses due to vacancies. Generally speaking, the break-even point is 80-percent occupancy for buildings and shopping centers, and slightly less—about 75 percent—for industrial space. Sound planning calls for a certain portion of rental income (generally 10 percent) to be set aside as "vacancy reserves," to guard against losses due to vacancies. Other risks include changes in population or the quality of the neighborhood, obsolescence, poor management, and regulatory or rezoning problems.

Cashing In on the Ground Floor

If you already own a business in town, you can easily build a small commercial real estate operation based on your reputation. Lenders like to lend to businesspeople they know, and you'll discover you can get financing more quickly than an outsider. Ask local attorneys and real estate brokers to tell you about their commercial deals. For example, a lawyer disposing of property for an estate may then call you first; the same can be true of brokers. Talk to these professionals on a regular basis and let them know you're interested.

If you live near your commercial property, management headaches are far fewer, too. Hire local people, even relatives, to oversee your investment.

Study your area's growth patterns. Is business moving to the south end of town? Buy there before the rest!

Find out about new businesses. Listen to your friends, your banker and lawyer—everyone. Is a new shopping mall coming in? Is a chain store corporation or a hotel moving to town? Get details by going to the source and then seek out nearby property. Put down an option to buy while you watch the area develop. If you're wrong, you lose that amount, but if you're right your option money goes toward the down payment on the property.

Watch zoning changes carefully. Attend all zoning board meetings or send someone in your place. When a property changes from residential to commercial, you might get a jump on everyone else— and that's how to make money in real estate.

TWELVE TERMS YOU MUST KNOW

After-tax cash flow: The spendable income from the investment after income taxes.

Anchor tenant: A major chain, corporation, or store that generates traffic for smaller stores in a shopping center; also called a "magnet" store.

Cash flow: The process of collecting income or revenues and paying for expenses, capital additions, or major repairs. This flow of money in and out results in a net profit or loss.

Depreciation: The gradual real or theoretical dimunition in value of a property (although not land) over time due to wear and tear; it is a tax-deductible expense for those investing in business or commercial property.

Net lease: The lessee assumes responsibility for paying operating expenses of the property (excluding capital expenditures); that means the rent received by the lessor is all net to the lessor.

Net operating income: Balance remaining after operating expenses are subtracted from gross rental income. In contrast to cash flow, net operating income is arrived at without deduction for debt service on any mortgage or capital improvements.

Operating expenses: The day-to-day costs related to income-producing properties. These expenses include: taxes, utilities, insurance, and management fees.

Percentage lease: Total rent paid by tenant varies based upon business done by the tenant; usually determined by gross sales or receipts.

Reappraisal lease: Rent is reappraised at periodic intervals during its life; normally used only in very long-term leases.

Replacement reserve: A fund established by owner for covering replacement of property — usually for such items as furniture, carpeting, roofs, paving, and appliances.

Sale leaseback: An arrangement whereby an owner-occupant sells property to an investor and at the same time executes a lease to continue to occupy the property on mutually agreeable terms; this provides immediate rental income to the investor.

Triple-net lease: Also known as a net-net-net lease. Here the tenant is responsible for expenses including real estate taxes, capital improvements, etc.

Community Assemblages

If your property lies in the path of change, it may mean big money for you. Residential areas that have become less desirable due to urbanization are candidates today for "assemblages" — real estate-eze for the sale of whole subdivisions of houses or geographical areas as one unit to a large commercial developer.

Your neighborhood's chances of being sold as an assemblage are greater if: 1) it's located in an area being considered for an office development, shopping mall or other commercial undertaking; 2) it's near or in the way of an interstate highway; 3) there's enough land involved—5 to 40 acres; and 4) it's located in an underbuilt area.

If you suspect you live in a potential assemblage, check with a commercial real estate broker or marketing firm. If the answer is yes, then sound out your neighbors, initially by letter, followed up by a phone call, and finally a neighborhood meeting. If the majority of the neighbors favor selling out, then elect a committee to handle the negotiations, and hire a real estate attorney.

All the neighbors will be asked to sign a legal document indicating they will sell as a group. If several people decide not to join in, the plan can still proceed since architects work around most such obstacles. The document should also spell out how the proceeds of the sale will be divided, with those owning more expensive homes receiving greater dollar amounts. In the recent Peachtree-Dunwoody Valley sale, involving 45 homes outside Atlanta, sellers received an equal number of dollars for each square foot of land they owned. And in Arlington, VA, 22 homeowners reached agreement to sell their six acres in a single parcel for approximately $10 million. Another item to include in the document is the minimum price the group will accept and how long that price will remain firm.

Other points to work out with a lawyer include:

- **Financing Terms.** Will it be an all-cash deal or will the group accept a mortgage?

- **Rezoning.** If you and your neighbors can get the area rezoned for commercial use prior to selling, you can set a higher price on your property; otherwise, obtaining offers will be contingent on obtaining rezoning. Lobbying for such a change is time-consuming but important, and becomes the responsibility of your steering committee. The buyer or potential buyer can petition for rezoning, too, but you're likely to get a lower price than if rezoning is already accomplished.

- **Moving Property.** List any buildings, trees, plants, etc., that may be moved by the homeowners prior to the sale.

Once the group is prepared to sell, have a real estate broker prepare a prospectus, which includes a map, site description, demographic studies, zoning rules, market analysis, etc. The prospectus should then be distributed to all potentially interested developers. A reliable broker will know who the best developers are and should steer you away from those with a poor reputation.

Although "assemblage" real estate is a relatively new concept, the cases to date have been extremely successful, with homeowners all receiving far more than would have been possible had they sold as individuals. However, if for some reason you decide not to participate in an assemblage affecting your neighborhood, make sure you consult a lawyer—but not the group's lawyer.

BECOME AN EXPERT

For further information, contact:

- DeRand Realty Corp.
  Arlington, VA
  703-527-3827

9 Investing with Family Help

Nearly one third of all houses purchased by first-time buyers today are partially financed with help from a family member. Parents, grandparents, and rich uncles often play a crucial role in the world of real estate. But before getting or giving family help, be sure to know the facts—even between loving relatives, misunderstandings over money often arise. Protect yourself ahead of time.

There are four basic ways to help relatives or be helped by them:

Gifts. An outright gift, instead of a loan, is the least complicated way to become involved. For the giver this has the advantage of reducing estate taxes, and for both parties there are generally no strings attached. You can give up to $10,000 away per person each year with no gift tax whatsoever involved for either party. That means, for example, that each of two parents can give $10,000 to their daughter and $10,000 to their son-in-law, for a total tax-free gift to the couple of $40,000. If both sets of parents chip in, this could reach $80,000! (Lenders frequently require that parents write an official letter verifying the fact that this money is indeed a gift and not a loan in disguise.) In some states, however, there may be restrictions due to state gift tax regulations; be sure to find out what the laws are where you live.

Loans. Provided certain circumstances prevail, Uncle Sam may let relatives lend you up to $100,000 interest-free. Be sure to consult your accountant about how to structure such a loan. Both you and the lender might be subject to certain taxes relating to the loan.

Mortgages. You can ask a relative to cosign your mortgage, but remember, if you default on the payments, you will be leaving them 100-percent liable. Although cosigning often enables you to obtain a mortgage you might not otherwise receive, it also places a burden on your relatives. If you do not keep up your payments, the cosigner's signature could make them liable for the monthly mortgage payments; otherwise, foreclosure could take place.

Equity Sharing. If you make enough money to cover your monthly mortgage payments plus upkeep of the house, but you don't have the cash for the down payment, equity sharing is a popular solution. In a shared equity mortgage, parents become the co-owners of their child's house and also help make mortgage payments. By becoming co-owners the parents get certain tax breaks, such as depreciation, and deductions for interest payments and real estate taxes. For example, your parents might agree to put up 50 percent of the down payment in exchange for 50 percent ownership of the property. Then, you and your parents divide the monthly mortgage payments, insurance, and taxes—and you share the tax benefits as well. Generally, the child assumes maintenance costs, but this is something you'll have to work out directly with your parents, and arrangements may vary from case to case. At the same time, you pay a fair market rental on your share to your parents. This point is crucial, for in order to protect your parents' right to take depreciation in a shared equity venture, they must charge a "fair market rent" for the proportion of the house that you do not own but are living in. That means that even if parents assume half the mortgage payments, most of the rest is still going to be paid by you, but in the form of rent.

A Trap to Avoid. If you and your parents have a 50-50 deal and if the rent is equal to half the mortgage payment, then you are actually paying the equivalent of the full mortgage but will not get the full benefits of property tax and interest deductions; you'll only get half of these benefits. In this case, you might be better off with one of the other family arrangements discussed, such as a gift. Then you would be eligible for a greater share of the tax breaks.

If you participate in equity sharing, mortgage cosigning, or loans, treat them as business transactions. Have a real estate attorney draw up the appropriate papers clarifying who is responsible for what, how long the transaction will last, and, most importantly, what will happen if one or the other of you defaults, dies, or wants out. And remember, never ask a family member to deplete their own nest egg to help build yours.

BECOME AN EXPERT

The following companies have basic real estate contract forms that can be used by those entering into shared real estate ventures. Most have modifications to accommodate individual state laws.

- Prescott Forbes Group
  260 South Broad Street
  Philadelphia, PA 19102
  215-751-0486

- Shared Equity Specialists
  819 Silver Spring Avenue
  Silver Spring, MD 20910
  301-587-0867

- Ticket Corporation
  233 Brookcliff Trace
  Marietta, GA 30068
  404-973-9474

Renting to Family

You can help your children, aging parents or others in your family with housing, and at the same time reap profits and tax benefits. Here's how it works: You buy a co-op or house, rent to a family member at fair market value, and in exchange you'll be able to take advantage of the usual rental tax breaks, as explained below. Later on, when your child moves on or your parents die, hopefully you'll be able to sell at a higher price than you paid. (Or, if you like, you can continue to rent it out or even move in yourself.) It's basically a painless way to lend a helping hand.

"Kiddie Condos" for College Students

Most students live in a dorm, in college-owned off-campus housing, or they rent space nearby. But if you want to stop paying hefty dorm fees, which merely go down the drain, consider buying a condo or a small house for your student to live in. As a property owner, you will have the standard tax benefits — deduction of mortgage interest and property taxes — plus a host of other tax breaks that accompany ownership of rental property, regardless of whether your rental property is a primary or secondary residence. It is important to note, however, that in order to qualify for tax breaks associated with rentals you *must* charge your relative a fair market rate. Otherwise your arrangement won't qualify as a true "rental" with the IRS.

These tax breaks are:

Depreciation. You can deduct part of the cost each year for 27.5 years (see Appendix).

Maintenance. If your child pays you a fair market rent from his own funds, then your maintenance expenses (such as utilities and repairs) are deductible, since the IRS views the transaction as rental property. (If your student does not pay rent to you, then costs associated with maintenance are not deductible.)

Salary. Here's another way to turn your rental real estate to your advantage. Hire your own student son or daughter to manage the property (i.e., mow the lawn, do repairs, etc.). If more than one unit is involved, your child can act as rental agent — for getting other students to share or even for renting out to summer school students. The salary you pay can be deducted from the taxable rental income. And, because you've effectively shifted some of your income to your child, taxes on this income will be paid at a lower rate, since children are usually in a lower tax bracket than their parents.

If the expenses connected with your property are more than the rental income, you can deduct up to $25,000 of the excess as a loss. However, if your income is above the $100,000 mark, this deduction is reduced and eliminated altogether after $150,000. Check with your accountant for specific advice.

The Risks Involved

Housing near college campuses is almost always expensive, but the farther away you go the less you'll have to pay. But then your student may need a car, adding to the cost of the whole venture. In addition, college students are not known to be the best tenants, which means mortgage loans for "kiddie condos" are becoming increasingly difficult to obtain. Another potential problem, of course, is that your student may leave college or transfer, leaving you with a sizable investment on your hands.

To reduce these and other risks, and to make the deal profitable, buy college housing for rental purposes only if:

- You or you child will live in the area after graduation

- You can rent to others besides your child

- You have more than one child going to the same school

- You can buy in an area where there's not a kiddie condo glut

- You can buy near campus or near sorority or fraternity houses that provide a built-in group of renters

- Your son or daughter is responsible enough to handle a rental

Grannie Maes

At some point you may need to help your parents or grandparents with their housing arrangements. They may need additional income if they are retired and living on a fixed income. One way to help them and take a tax deduction at the same time is to buy their home and then rent it back to them. This family sale-leaseback plan — commonly referred to as a "Grannie Mae" — provides your parents or grandparents with a large sum of money, either to invest or live on. And, of course, it gives you the various tax breaks that accompany rental income, including deductions for mortgage interest, real estate taxes, depreciation, and maintenance costs.

A variation on this arrangement can help you buy your first home, even if you have little money saved. If your parents need steady income but not a lump sum, then you don't make a down payment on their house. Instead you purchase the house through large monthly payments. Your parents, in turn, pay you a fair market rent, but one that is less than the amount they're receiving from you.

Reverse Annuity Mortgages

Another approach is to have your parents purchase a reverse annuity mortgage, known as a RAM. This is an ideal solution for house-rich folks who are income-poor or cash-shy. Here's an example of how it could work:

Your parents' house is mortgage-clear or has only a small amount left due. It's worth $100,000, but they will realize this value only if it is sold, which they are reluctant to do. In lieu of selling, they borrow against the house, using it as collateral. They arrange with a bank to get a RAM—the bank might lend them, for example, 80 percent of the value of the property over a 10-year period. Your parents will receive the payments in monthly installments, thus giving them a new steady stream of income.

At the end of the mortgage time period, your parents will have a mortgage against their house, but during that same interval the house will have appreciated in value. They then face two options. One is to sell the house and pay off the mortgage; the other is to refinance the house through another RAM.

Similar annuity arrangements are available from many insurance companies. Before either buying your parents' house or encouraging them to get a RAM, talk to your accountant about these possibilities. This type of decision should be part of their overall estate planning and should *not* be made without professional guidance.

Tax Benefit: Parents can take advantage of the once-in-a-lifetime real estate tax exemption: If the homeseller is age 55 or over, he has a one-time exclusion that permits him to escape paying tax on the first $125,000 of profit, whether or not he then buys another home.

10 Bed & Breakfast

A ll across the nation, American homeowners are making extra cash by opening their homes to the traveling public as "bed and breakfasts." Although traditionally a European institution, "B&Bs" are increasingly becoming part of the American landscape as young couples, country folk, and city slickers find a way to pay the mortgage and have fun at the same time.

Today there are over 10,000 B&Bs in the United States, just about double the number in existence in 1980. They offer a homey atmosphere, personal attention, and modest prices—a combination that's hard to beat. Although most are country inns and traditional guest houses, B&Bs are popping up wherever there's a spare bedroom—in apartments, condos, and even city lofts.

Getting Started

Step 1: Before you rent out your married children's bedrooms, you should decide if you want to run your B&B as a full-time business, or as a sideline or hobby to make sound use of those empty spaces. You must also consider your location: Does it have year-round appeal for travelers, or is it seasonal—perfect only during ski months, holidays, swim season, or fall foliage time? It's also wise to discuss the conversion of the old homestead with other members of the family before going ahead with your plans.

Step 2: Determine local zoning laws. Small B&Bs are often able to open with little legal hassle, whereas larger establishments providing shelter for many people fall under the "commercial" category and therefore must meet zoning and public health requirements. Check with your local zoning board.

Step 3: Initial "start-up" expenses should be determined ahead of time, of course, but with care they can be kept to a minimum. Among the costs you must figure on are: insurance, printing and/or advertising, fire alarm systems and any other equipment required by local ordinances. Insurance at a reduced rate is offered for members of the trade association, Bed and Breakfast, U.S.A., Ltd. A $1,000,000 liability policy is available for $150 per year plus $50 per room for over three rooms. A comparable policy purchased independently would be much costlier — possibly as much as $1,000.

Step 4: Determining rates is the name of the game. Your rate will depend on the accommodations you offer, of course, as well as on the kind of breakfast you serve. (Despite their name, not all B&Bs include breakfast in the price of the room!) Most B&Bs charge 30 to 40 percent less than regular hotels in the same vicinity. An additional charge — $10, perhaps — can be added on for a private bath. Browse through the guidebooks for help in setting your rates (see "Become an Expert," below).

Step 5: Your brochure and cards should be artistically designed. People who prefer B&Bs over traditional hotels are often history or architecture buffs, and you'll want to appeal to their sense of aesthetics. A unique feature, such as gingerbread trim, stained glass, or a wrought-iron gate should be represented on your flyer, along with rates, number of available rooms, bathrooms, special services and meals offered, minimum length of stay, cancellation policy, and a reservation form.

Step 6: When you are ready to open your doors, send your brochures to nearby schools and colleges, corporations, caterers, the Chamber of Commerce, bus and train stations, airports, and libraries. You can also extend your coverage by joining an official reservation system. Most charge annual dues ranging from $25 to upwards of $100, plus a 20 percent commission. They will list your establishment in their directory, advertise, handle confirmations, and in many cases pre-screen guests. (This last service alone may be well worth the cost involved, since you'll be opening your own home — and giving your keys — to strangers.)

BECOME AN EXPERT

The following associations and publications will provide you with a wealth of helpful information:

- Bed and Breakfast, U.S.A., Ltd. (trade association;
  can assist with reservations)
  P.O. Box 606
  Croton-on-Hudson, NY 10520

- *Open Your Home as a Bed and Breakfast,* by Barbara Notarius (published by John Wiley Publishers, New York, 1987)

- *Bed and Breakfast, U.S.A.,* by Betty Runback and Nancy Kramer (published annually by E.P. Dutton, Inc., New York)

- The Learning Annex and local YWCAs and YMCAs offer courses in major U.S. cities

11 Renting to the Movies

You may not realize it, but your house, farm, or cottage may be a star, waiting in the wings to be discovered. It's surprisingly easy and exceptionally profitable to rent your place to movie and television producers or to advertising agencies for commercials. Many pay as much as $1,000 per day to shoot live scenes inside your house or on the grounds.

You're most likely to catch a director's attention if your property has something unusual, such as a gabled attic, mansion-sized space, period details (stained glass, fireplaces, molding, circular staircases), an eat-in or large country kitchen, or a large laundry room. Maybe you have exceptional views, a stream or lake, a hayloft, a tennis court, or a location on an interesting street. A decorator's touch can add allure—Laura Ashley fabrics, chintz, and the Art Deco look are "in" right now.

Filmmakers are required to clear projects with the municipal film commission, so your first step should be to list your property with your area's commission, either at the state or town level. This is a way both to make yourself known to filmmakers and to find out about films and commercials that will be shot in your area. Check your telephone book or call your city hall to find out where the local film commission is located.

Second, register with one of the national services that matches property with directors. Below is a partial list of those maintaining photo files of houses. The producer, not you, pays the finder's fee. Call first for details; then send pictures that highlight your property's unique features.

FILM SERVICES		
Name	**City**	**Telephone**
Judie Robbins Locations	New York, NY	212-391-4970
Location Locators	New York, NY	212-685-6363
Location Connection	New York, NY	212-481-9111
Wild Locations	New York, NY	212-391-6647
Locations Unlimited	Tenafly, NJ	201-567-2809
Cast Locations	Los Angeles, CA	213-469-6616

The Risks Involved

This is not an activity for the fussy or the weak-minded. If you don't want lots of people running about your kitchen, don't get involved. As many as 50 to 100 people may show up to film one scene of a movie, less for a TV commercial. Add to that the caterers, trucks, equipment, and noise—all of which will disrupt your routine and invade your privacy.

Some producers may move your furniture or put it in storage; others will rewallpaper or paint your livingroom. If it's a long project, the company may put you up in a hotel.

The Contract

You can protect your "star" property or house through a well-drawn contract. If your lawyer is not involved in the drafting of the contract, be sure he or she reviews it thoroughly. Among the items that should be included are:

- Restoration to previous condition
- Filming dates

- Restitution for damages and/or theft
- Liability for personal injury
- Floor refinishing, rug cleaning, and any other household repairs that must be made
- Your name in the credits.

PART THREE

Leisure-Time Real Estate

Once you've purchased your first home and watched it appreciate in value, you'll be ready to use the equity you've built up and add to your success — this time with vacation property. Or, if you're an apartment dweller who rents, then it's all the more important to establish yourself in the lucrative world of real estate. And, what could be more fun than having a place of your own to escape to on weekends, holidays, and during the summer months?

Most vacation or leisure homes — whether a tiny seaside cottage or an old-fashioned farmhouse — also lend themselves to being rented out for substantial sums, thus offering the dual benefits of tax write-offs *and* income.

For outdoor types there's healthy exercise as well as money in working farmland, planting timber, raising cows, or growing pecans. Or, if you're a history buff, then you can have fun rehabilitating an old building in your spare time and capturing the hefty tax credit offered by the government to those who adhere to federal rehab guidelines.

In the following pages you'll find everything you need to know about choosing, financing, and enjoying all sorts of leisure-time property.

12 | Making a Vacation Home Pay Off

Interest rates are low, mortgages are readily available, gasoline is cheap, and tax benefits still exist (see page 2), in spite of the new law. A number of vacation areas are overbuilt, the markets glutted with unsold condos and houses. All in all, this is an excellent time to buy a money-making vacation home.

So, if you've always dreamed of owning a beach cottage, a mountain lodge, or a ski chalet, there may be no better time to make that dream come true. Contrary to popular opinion, vacation homes are no longer a luxury available only to the very rich. According to the National Association of Home Builders, the average value of a second home is $71,100, versus $80,300 for a primary single-family residence. Condos, generally newer, are $95,000 or more (regardless of whether they are primary or secondary residences). Believe it or not, there *are* ways to make the purchase of a vacation home affordable, without giving up a good night's sleep.

Location

Your first consideration, even more important than price, should be location—as it should be with any piece of real estate. Do you love lakes, woods, rivers, or the ocean? Tennis, canoeing, skiing, or swimming? You certainly want a place that you and your family will be sure to use and yet that also has good resale value. A tiny cabin way up in the woods far from civilization may be perfect for you and your fishing buddies, but it's doubtful as an investment, except perhaps as a *very* long-term commitment. For resale value, think instead of a house with a modern kitchen and bath in an area with good restaurants and sports facilities, and within an easy drive of a city. A remote mountain retreat—lovely though it may be—could be difficult to unload when you're ready to sell.

The most popular vacation spots have remained the same for some time: southern Florida, eastern Long Island, Cape Cod, the New Jersey shore, and the southern California desert. Currently growing in appeal are ski resorts and lakes. The best investments are those in areas that cannot be replicated—houses near the ocean or at a ski resort. Lakefront property is also prized, while golf courses and planned communities hold somewhat less value. Of course, the closer you are to the ocean, ski lift, or lake, the more you will pay—and the more you'll be able to sell for down the line.

SAMPLING OF PROPERTIES

Key West, FL	New condo on ocean	$225,000
Monadnock Lake, NH	House with water view	$150,000
North Padres Island, TX	Condo on canal	$120,000
	Condo on beach	$ 95,000
Puget Sound, WA	House on water	$200,000
Phoenix, AZ	Townhouse	$135,000
East Hampton, NY	House near ocean	$1,000,000
	House in woods	$275,000
Seabrook Island, SC	Condo	$160,000
Palm Springs, CA	Condo	$125,000
Aspen, CO	House	$350,000
	Condo	$200,000
Pioneer Lake, WI	Waterfront house	$165,000

(All prices for a two-bedroom home)

A vacation home should be in a community that's an easy drive from a major metropolitan area, a maximum of four hours. Otherwise, prospective buyers and renters will not consider it as a weekend place. Look also for an area that is zoned against business or further development.

Bidding. Once you've located the property, the bargaining begins. If the area is overbuilt, a good rule of thumb is to bid 20 percent less than the asking price. (If the area is *not* overbuilt, you'll have to bid much closer to the asking price.) Find out if the owner is willing to help finance the purchase; if so, you may be able to save as much as two percent over a bank mortgage.

Making It Affordable

There are several techniques that make it possible to cut costs and afford the seemingly unaffordable:

- **Buying with a Friend.** If you're hard pressed to swing a vacation home, you may want to buy with a friend, a family member, or another potential buyer. It can dramatically reduce your expenses, usually by 50 percent. (The details of shared ownership are explained in full in Chapter 24.) The inherent problems in sharing are far less troublesome in a vacation home than in a primary residence, since you can split use of the space by weekends, by weeks, or even by months, thus ensuring everyone more privacy.

- **Refinancing.** If you already own a home you may be able to refinance it at a lower interest rate than you are currently paying. This will free up money to use toward a down payment on your vacation home. (Details on refinancing are given in Chapter 24.) Keep in mind that most lenders will give up to 80 percent of a house's appraised value in a mortgage. To determine how much you can get through refinancing, multiply .80 (80 percent) by the market value of your house. Then subtract your current mortgage obligation to arrive at the dollar amount you may receive.

- **Renting.** This is another excellent way to reduce the costs of carrying a vacation home. In addition, if you rent out your vacation home for long-enough time periods, you'll qualify for the tax deductions detailed below.

Tax Considerations

The 1986 Tax Reform Act preserved some of the benefits traditionally associated with homeownership, such as mortgage interest deductions on your first and second home, along with deduction of property taxes. But homeowners who rent out a vacation home have new rules to follow.

Prior to tax reform, if you used your vacation home for two weeks or less, you were allowed to deduct rental expenses such as utilities, depreciation, and maintenance *even* if they were greater than your rental income.

Residential vs. Rental Vacation Property

Under the new law, the size of allowable deductions—assuming that you own at least 10 percent of the property—is determined by whether your home is classified as "residential" or "rental" property, by how large your gross income is, and by whether or not you actively manage the property.

Your vacation home will be considered a "residence" by the IRS if your personal use exceeds 14 days or (if you rent it out) a period longer than 10 percent of the number of days it's rented, whichever is greater. If, on the other hand, your personal use of your vacation home is *less* than 15 days, and you rent it out for 15 days or more, this home qualifies as a regular "rental" property. Federal tax laws differ for each of these two categories:

Residential Vacation Homes:

- If you rent for less than 15 days, you may *not* deduct any expenses attributed to the rental except for mortgage interest, real estate taxes, and casualty losses (financial losses caused by the sudden or unexpected damage, destruction, or loss of property). If you make a profit on this rental, it is *not* taxed.

- If you rent for 15 days or more and if your personal use exceeds 14 days or 10 percent of the time rented, then rental expenses on the home are deductible *only* up to an amount equal to the total rental income you receive from it. In other words, you can deduct your mortgage interest, property taxes, and expenses, as long as the total of these is not greater than your rental income. (In some cases, you may be able to deduct mortgage interest and real estate taxes if they are in excess of rental income; check with your accountant.)

Rental Vacation Homes:

- If you rent for 15 days or more and your personal use is less than the 14-day/10-percent test, expenses *in excess of rental income* are deductible within IRS guidelines for regular rental property. Guidelines for rental property are complex, however, and you should check with your accountant for details. It's important to know that, *in general*, expenses and income from rental property are considered "passive" (see page 3), and as such, losses can only be used to offset income from other passive investments, currently or in the future.

In both residential and rental situations, you cannot deduct expenses for days you spend there yourself or for days when the home is rented by anyone who does not pay the going market rate.

There are some exceptions that allow you to increase your current deductions, and they are designed to help the small real estate investor. If your vacation home qualifies as a rental property, you can deduct up to $25,000 of rental losses (the amount of rental expenses that is in excess of total rental revenue) annually, as long as you meet three conditions: 1) you own at least 10 percent of the property; 2) you actively manage the property; and 3) your adjusted gross income is less than $100,000. (Points 1 and 2 apply more specifically to investors involved in greater numbers of rental units.)

If you rent out part of your *primary residence* as vacation space for more than 15 days a year, and you meet the three conditions outlined above, you can also deduct current tax losses up to the $25,000 limit for the rented portion of your home. You cannot deduct any rental losses, however, for a vacation home that qualifies as a residence with the IRS (as defined above) if it is *not* your primary residence.

For adjusted gross incomes over $100,000, this $25,000 limit is gradually phased out, so that by the time your income reaches $150,000, none of the $25,000 is currently deductible.

Any allowable losses that are not currently deductible may be carried forward until they can be used against passive income.

13 Vacation Time Shares

If you've dreamed of a luxury vacation every year but lack the dollars to buy a condo in Spain or a house in Palm Beach, you should look into real estate time sharing. It's a way to enter the vacation scene inexpensively and at the same time save on leisure-time dollars in your budget.

Time sharing, which came into vogue in the 1960s in the French Alps, is a way to guarantee space at a resort for a particular time every year. Each unit — a room, apartment, condo, or individual house — is divided into intervals, frequently by weeks, and these intervals are sold separately to vacationers.

Approximately half the time shares in the U.S. are sold on a "floating" basis, which provides a degree of flexibility in selecting the weeks that are yours every year.

How Time Shares Work

Prices. The cost of ownership is based on the property's location, its size, the time of year your time share is to be used, and the various facilities offered. For example, the winter weeks in a Florida condo will cost much more than in July and August. Since a time-shared resort is owned jointly by all the purchasers, owners pay yearly maintenance fees in addition to their basic costs. Prices for time shares range from $2,000 to $20,000, with most under $10,000. Vacationers who don't participate in time-shared ownership typically pay almost twice that much to rent the same accommodations during the same time period.

Mortgages are difficult to obtain for time shares, but you can often get financing through a personal loan from the developer. You must come up with the 10 percent down payment, and the rest can be paid off over 5 to 10 years. When mortgages are granted, the time share is generally used as collateral.

Advantages. The key advantage to time sharing is that you wind up paying only for the actual time you use your space. Because units come equipped with a kitchen, you also save by eating at least some of your meals at home. Although your unit may indeed appreciate in value, this is not always the case. So, buy with the idea in mind that you will save on the amount you generally budget for your vacation and that you may be able to sublet your unit if you elect not to use it. Subletting is subject to the bylaws of the co-op or condo association in most cases.

Note: If you have a mortgage on your unit, the interest is tax deductible. And, depending upon your particular arrangement, if you pay property taxes, those, too are deductible. Should you rent out your time share, consult Chapter 7 regarding tax benefits on rental property.

Disadvantages. A time share should not be viewed as a way to make money fast. Reselling quickly at a profit seldom works, especially if the resort is new and the developer is still in the process of selling units. The price of your unit may also be inflated above true market value because of the developer's heavy promotional costs. Resale value frequently improves with time, however. A $7,000 unit may not appreciate during the first four to five years but then could bring $10,000, depending upon the market and inflation rate. If you're particularly interested in quick appreciation, investigate "fractional ownership," which is described later in this section. Administrative costs for fractional units are far lower, so your investment appreciates more rapidly.

The Risk Involved

The entire time-share industry has been plagued in the past by problems which lead many people to be cautious about investing, and rightfully so. Even now, you cannot be too careful, although most of the early kinks have been ironed out. The recent entry into the field by large real estate firms—such as Holiday Corporation, Marriott, and ITT—has given increased credibility to the time-share concept. In the early days, lack of experience, poor regulation, and some fly-by-night speculators caused great difficulties and gave time shares some very bad press.

Today, however, most states regulate the industry and require developers to make public disclosure of their plans and financial status. In addition, they must place all buyers' payments in escrow accounts and give them up to 15 days to back out of their purchase. In a number of states, local and state regulators continually investigate time-share resorts that appear to lack adequate financing. Those with "come-on" promotional gimmicks have also been barred from doing business in some areas. You should, of course, check with your state attorney general's office to see if any such firms have previously been prevented from selling in your area. A time-share resort in Florida, for example, may not be allowed to promote sales or close deals outside of Florida.

Yet time sharing can be not only a happy but a sound investment; you can avoid disillusionment *if* you don't rush in and make a quick decision without proper information and investigation. Fortunately, there are a number of reputable sources to turn to. Among the better-known companies are: York-Hanovers Development of Toronto; U.S. Fairfield Communities of Little Rock; the Marriott Corporation; and Divi Hotels.

Types of Plans

A time share may be for a furnished studio, a suite, a condo, a cottage, or an attached home. There are two basic ways to buy one:

1) Fee Simple (also known as Interval Ownership). In return for a one-time purchase plus an annual maintenance fee, you receive a legal title, deed, and title insurance for a fraction of the property (i.e., your unit), plus ownership of your interval (i.e., your week or weeks). In other words, you maintain ownership in perpetuity— without a time limitation. You generally can sell, rent, or will the unit to heirs or others. You pay property tax in the fee simple plan, which can be deducted from your income tax.

In a fee simple time share you automatically join an owner's association, which takes control of the resort when most units or weeks are sold. The association may or may not choose to keep on the developer as manager. If the developer has been assessing realistic annual fees all along, then there should be an adequate maintenance fund. Some developers, unfortunately, charge artificially low fees in order to boost sales, and end up turning over a poorly financed setup.

2) Right to Use. If you can't quite afford fee-simple owner-ship—or if you're not sure it's for you—a smaller payment will entitle you to exclusive occupancy rights for a set number of years (usually 12 to 40) for a given unit. However, you do not own the unit in this arrangement, and at the end of the time period your rights expire (although they can be renewed by additional payment in most cases). You may or may not be able to sublet or sell your unit. (*Note:* In the "right-to-use" plan, ask for a "non-disturbance" clause that allows you to retain your rights should the seller default. Not every management will grant your request, but it's well worth fighting for.)

SELECTING A TIME SHARE

- Never buy without visiting the property first; talk to other time sharers regarding services, etc.

- Read the literature, especially the prospectus; check the facts with your accountant.

- Buy from an established firm that's well capitalized.

- Check the firm's references with its lender, the state attorney general, the local chamber of commerce, and the Better Business Bureau.

- Read the sales contract for an explanation of your rights if the resort has difficulties.

- In the disclosure statement, see if there is an adequate maintenance fund. The developer should contribute to this fund for all units not sold.

- Don't sign any contract unless it contains a clause giving you a minimum of one to two weeks to change your mind, without incurring a penalty.

- Before signing on the dotted line, check to see if there's a "resale" agent who handles units at the same resort. If so, you may be able to get a lower price on a comparable unit.

- Once you've made your purchase, call the county clerk in the area where your unit is located to make certain your title has been properly recorded.

- Be wary of low maintenance fees. Hefty assessments may follow.

- If the unit is unfinished, get a written guarantee that it will be completed, and by a certain date. Ask your accountant or lawyer if your payment should be held in escrow until completion.

Fractional Ownership

A new alternative to the traditional time-share arrangement is fractional ownership, which allows you to buy a larger chunk of time. The most popular version is the quarter-ownership plan, in which the unit is divided into four separate three-months deeds. Ten- and five-week plans also exist. Fractional ownership is close to actually purchasing a vacation home because the amount of time you have is so much greater than the one or two weeks per year associated with regular time shares. Its costs are also higher, with many falling into the $50,000 category. But, if you were to buy an equivalent time period in smaller units of time, it would probably cost more.

As in a time share, the fractional ownership's management company is responsible for all maintenance, inside and out. It pays for the electricity and utilities, and handles rental of units when not used by the owners. Each owner uses the property every fourth week, with the sequence moving forward one week every year to give all owners a chance at the "best" times.

Fractional ownership is particularly successful because it fills a gap in the vacation market between time shares, which offer short vacation periods, and full ownership.

Appreciation is faster than with time shares, primarily because administrative and promotional costs are lower since each unit does not have to be rented out 52 times a year. In fact, markup in price to cover these costs is occasionally zero.

If you decide to sell your time share, you have several options: You may be able to do so through your managing agent, by advertising in local or city newspapers, or through one of the larger services listed below. But, *don't expect to make a killing*—time shares usually do appreciate in value over a long period of time, but for short-term investments, you'll do better with a single-family vacation home.

TIME SHARE RESALE AGENTS

- Holiday Condominiums
  7701 Pacific St.
  Omaha, NB 68114
  800-228-0002

- RE/MAX MDR
  13470 Washington Blvd.
  Marina del Rey, CA 90292
  800-423-6377
  213-821-0452 in California

Exchange Plans

If your resort belongs to an exchange network, you may be able to trade your week for a week somewhere else. Dues are usually $50 per year, plus $50 per exchange. Many networks also levy a one-time membership fee of up to $250. Two of the largest exchange networks are: Resort Condominiums International, P.O. Box 80229, Indianapolis, IN 46240 (317-876-8899); and Interval International, 7000 S.W. 62nd Avenue, Miami, FL 33143 (800-828-8200 or 800-462-8408 in New York State).

BECOME AN EXPERT

For additional information, contact:

- National Timeshare Council
  1220 L St., N.W.
  Washington, DC 20005
  202-371-6700

A free copy of *Ten Timeshare Tips* is available from:

- Federal Trade Commission
  Sixth and Pennsylvania Ave., N.W.
  Washington, DC 20580
  202-326-2000

14 Historic Rehabilitation

One of the best remaining tax breaks since the passage of the 1986 Tax Reform Act is the rehabilitation tax credit. Federal tax credits are provided by the government as an inducement to Americans to fix up old structures, thereby preserving our architectural heritage. This Investment Tax Credit (ITC) is 20 percent of the cost of rehabilitating historic buildings, or 10 percent for nonhistoric buildings built before 1936; it is generally claimed for the tax year in which the rehabilitation is completed. The 20-percent ITC provides a dollar-for-dollar reduction of income tax owed and applies only to rental buildings. Neither credit is available for homes or apartments occupied by their owners. In other words, the credit is available only for buildings used in business or held for producing rental income.

Certified Historic Structures: To qualify for the 20-percent ITC, a building must be listed individually in the National Register of Historic Places or located in a registered historic district and certified by the Secretary of the Interior as being of historical significance to the district.

Old Nonhistoric Buildings: A 10-percent rehabilitation credit is available for nonresidential, nonhistoric buildings built before 1936. For these buildings no certification is required to qualify for the tax credit.

Individual houses or districts can be designated historic on either a local or national level; they must first be nominated for historic certification by a local historic commission, *not* a renovation developer. The National Trust for Historic Preservation estimates that there are approximately 1,200 local historic commissions throughout the country. Before undertaking restoration of an old house, check with your local or state historic preservation office regarding the structure's designation. They will also supply you with information on approved restoration methods and building materials, as well as details on qualifying for the rehabilitation ITC. In addition, you should get a copy of the official guidelines from the Department of the Interior, Parks Service, P.O. Box 37127, Washington, DC 20013. (Ask for *Preservation: Tax Incentives for Historic Buildings*, and *Standards for Rehabilitation and Guidelines for Rehabilitating Historic Buildings*.)

Limited Partnerships

Even if you're not interested in rehabilitating a building or house on your own, you can still invest in America's architectural past through historic rehabilitation limited partnerships. Without them, the beautiful St. Louis Union Railroad Station would still be a shambles and Washington, DC's fashionable Willard Hotel a white elephant.

It all began in 1981 when Congress enacted a 25-percent tax credit (which was dropped to the current 20 percent in the 1986 Tax Reform Act) for developers who rehabilitate historic structures. Since that time, some 8.8 billion dollars have been invested in over 12,000 buildings throughout the country. Among the sites saved by the tax credit are a Danbury, Connecticut hat factory, now luxury apartments; Miami's Art Deco residential area; and the Lone Star Brewery in San Antonio, Texas, now an art museum. In addition, over 60,000 housing units have been saved and rehabilitated.

Limited partners investing in certified historic buildings—structures listed on the National Register of Historic Places—receive the same 20-percent tax credit as individuals investing on their own. All buildings must be income producing in order to qualify. As long as your adjusted gross income is under $200,000, you can use this tax credit to offset up to $25,000 of other income. For example, if, as a limited partner, you had $20,000 of qualified expenditures on a certified historic structure, you could offset 20 percent of taxes, or $4,000. (If your adjusted gross income is over $200,000, however, check with your accountant as to the advisability of investing in historic structures; it may not pay off.)

Publicly-sold limited partnerships are available from major brokerage firms and specialized developers. Minimum investments tend to be $2,500 or $5,000. Each sponsor will provide details on your potential return as well as tax benefits. Be prepared to hold your investment a minimum of six years to gain full tax benefits.

In limited partnerships the pools are either "blind," in which case you do not know what the specific project will be, or "semi-blind," if the buildings to be rehabilitated have been identified. Invest only with a well-financed, experienced developer. (See Chapter 17 for more details on limited partnerships.) Keep in mind that all rehab projects face a host of risks, such as unexpected construction costs, decertification, questionable rental market, etc.

Apart from the tax credits received, the appeal of rehab investments is also psychological and sentimental. Many people enjoy participating in saving old buildings. They are unique and cannot be duplicated in the marketplace, rents tend to be excellent, and they're frequently in prime locations.

PUBLIC PARTNERSHIPS

Historic Landmarks for
Living
Philadelphia, PA 19106
215-922-0900

Greater Boston
Development, Inc.
Boston, MA 02210
617-439-0072

Sterling Historic Securities
Manhasset, NY 11030
516-627-5223

The Lockwood Group
St. Louis, MO 63116
314-968-2205

HISTORIC REHABILITATION

For Whom

- Those interested in architectural restoration and rental property

Where to Purchase

- Shares of limited partnerships sold by stockbrokers and private sponsors

- If doing on your own, through local research

Minimum

- In a limited partnership: $2,500 to $5,000

- On your own: cost of actual rehabilitation work

Safety Factor

- Limited partnership: medium to high
- On your own: high

Advantages

- Investment tax credit
- Rental income plus potential appreciation
- Preservation of America's architectural heritage

Disadvantages

- Uncertainty regarding rehabilitation costs; may turn out to be higher than anticipated
- Tough guidelines for obtaining tax credit

15 Down on the Farm

If you believe in contrarian investing, now is the time to buy that Iowa cornfield. The sharp drop in the value of farmland, which began in 1980, continues to make national headlines. These declines have indeed been bittersweet—bitter for the families unable to make an adequate living from their farms, and sweet for the investors who want to buy while prices are still low.

Whereas in the past "gentleman farmers" often purchased acreage for tax benefits, with today's new tax rules and lower land prices, investors must think primarily in terms of income and possible long-term appreciation. Plan on five to ten years to double your investment. In the meantime, you'll receive a modest gain each year (say, two to five percent, and hopefully more, of your investment), along with some depreciation on buildings and equipment. And when the market rebounds, you'll be in a solid position to sell. No one is quite willing to predict precisely when farmland will go back up in value, but as land becomes rarer and rarer, prices will eventually rise. However, investing in farmland is suggested only for the patient.

A well-run operation will provide current cash returns. If you are an absentee investor, the share you receive is determined by the kind of lease arrangement you have with your tenant or manager. The four basic types are:

1) Cash-Rental Lease. The landlord rents his or her property, buildings, and any equipment at a flat rate, frequently on a per-acre basis. This approach eliminates many of the production risks and requires the least amount of involvement on the landlord's part. Production levels and market prices determine the dollar return to the tenant.

2) Share Agreement. The landlord's share of the farm's income is a given percentage of either the crop or livestock production. The landlord must participate in a portion of production costs. Most leases stipulate a 50-50 deal (e.g.,the landlord pays for half the seed, fertilizer, and chemical costs, and in return gets half the crop produced). The farmer pays no traditional "rent" in this arrangement.

3) Custom Arrangement. In this lease, the landlord accepts all the production risks and receives all the farm receipts. However, he contracts out all of the field work to "custom" operators.

4) Direct Arrangement. This is the most common lease method for large farms and ranches. The investor owns all the operating equipment, hires the necessary labor, and generally employs a residential manager who is salaried. The manager then assumes all operating responsibilities while the investor accepts the production risks along with all income.

Selecting a Farm

Begin by having a professional study the price, location, terms of agreement, and overall quality of the land involved. You will need the services of a real estate broker who deals primarily in farm properties, an attorney, an accountant, and a farm specialist. Among the quality tests the farm consultant should help you with are: soil, water, irrigation, conservation rules, mineral rights, labor pool, transportation facilities, and nearby markets for produce.

Management: A good manager—either a solo operator or an organization—must be equipped to offer: **1)** a three- to five-year plan; **2)** negotiation of leases; **3)** cash flow projections; **4)** budgets; **5)** periodic inspection reports; **6)** collection of rent or income; **7)** payment of bills; and **8)** an annual tax statement.

There are many local management firms throughout the nation. Check with the American Society of Farm Managers and Rural Appraisers, in Denver, CO (303-758-3513), for names in your area.

FARM BROKERS AND CONSULTANTS

Continental Bank & Trust
Chicago, IL
312-828-2345

Doane's Farm Management
St. Louis, MO
314-966-0761

Northern Trust Co.
Chicago, IL
312-630-6000

Oppenheimer Industries
Kansas City, MO
816-471-1750

The Risks Involved

There are a number of drawbacks to farming that you should note before rushing out to buy a farm of any kind:

- Income flow can be mercurial.

- Farming is subject to weather, floods, drought, disease, pests, etc.

- A farm is not a highly liquid holding.

- A farm should only be held as a long-term investment.

Timberland

You may have thought that only Hammermill, Scott Paper, and Weyerhaeuser Lumber Company invested in timberland. Not so. You too can get in on the action. In fact, the industry has so many small investors that they have formed their own trade group, the Forest Farmers Association. In the southern part of the country alone, there are an estimated one million privately owned timberlands, with parcels from as small as 50 acres on up to several thousand.

Timberland investments are competitive with bonds, stocks, and other types of real estate. From 1960 to 1985 they matched the compound rate of return of the Standard & Poor 500 Index—both were 9.2 percent. The return on long-term bonds over the same period was 6.2 percent; for other types of real estate, 8.5 percent.

To be successful as an investment, timberland lots generally should be at least 100 acres, and preferably more. Anything smaller may make it difficult to attract competitive bids from buyers, should you decide to sell.

Cost of Land

How much you will need to invest depends upon the location, condition, and size of the acreage you buy. For good quality basic land, cost per acre currently ranges from $150 to $350. You must then add on to that the expense of preparing the land and planting seedlings, which runs between $150 and $200 per acre. (These estimates vary widely from one section of the country to another. Check with your state forestry commission and real estate broker.)

In addition to the cost of land and seedlings, other items which must be factored in include annual taxes—about two dollars per acre per year—and periodic management expenses for thinning of trees, prescribed burning of land to get rid of competing vegetation, and maintaining boundary markers—about three dollars per acre per year.

If you enjoy the exercise and view yourself as a modern Paul Bunyan, you can clear away brush and mark your own trees, especially if you have a small acreage. If you're an indoor type or an absentee landlord, then a management company will care for your land and the sale of timber. A management company will also provide advice on what to plant when, as well as optimum harvest dates.

Income

Time is the critical factor in the tree business. The longer your investment is held, the less speculative it becomes. At an absolute minimum, plan on 35 years from the time you plant your saplings. Occasionally you will have to thin your land, which usually produces enough income to offset the expense of thinning that particular year. Most ongoing acreage, of course, has trees with varying maturities for producing a steady stream of income.

Although investing in timberland is a long-term commitment and not suggested for anyone in a hurry to make money, it has the great advantage of being a relatively trouble-free investment. You can be an absentee investor, and there's no hassle with repairs, finding good tenants, or overseeing the property.

BECOME AN EXPERT

Membership in the trade association costs $30/year and entitles you to free copies of *Forest Farmer*, a magazine devoted to timber management. The trade association also publishes *Forest Farmer Manual* (available for $15) every other year.

- Forest Farmers Association
  P.O. Box 95385
  Atlanta, GA 30347
  404-325-2954

Also, contact your local state forestry commission for additional information on buying and managing timberland.

Buying Raw Land

The ad reads: "One hundred acres, stream, part timberland, only $5,000 down and low, low monthly payment."

The dream of a lifetime? Possibly. But more likely an example of the old come-on that turns into a nightmare. Nowhere in the vast world of real estate have more innocent people been duped than in raw land deals, but it needn't happen to you. Buying land can be an excellent investment—people who purchased oceanfront acres 20 years ago have more than quadrupled their money. But those who put their faith and money in parts out West often came up with useless land in the middle of the desert.

Before you turn over a down payment to make your fortune in land, you and your lawyer must spend time researching the so-called "big six" questions, detailed below. Only when you have the answers to *all* six should you move ahead toward a purchase.

1) Access. Do you have access rights to the land? These should be permanent rights, transferable and specified in writing in the deed. If the land is on a county or state road, don't assume you can automatically put in a driveway; it depends on local laws and on your frontage (the number of feet you have along the road). If you eventually plan to develop the land and put in houses, the amount of frontage you have is crucial.

2) Water, Sewers, and Drainage. If there's a creek or a stream on the land, do you have the right to use it or is it part of a municipal watershed? If it's the latter, and you're planning to put livestock on the property, they too may be denied use of the water. Septic tanks are usually prohibited on watershed land as well. Don't buy until you receive written approval from the municipality regarding your rights to use of the water.

If the land you're considering needs a septic system in order to be habitable, the location of the tank will be determined by proximity to other water supplies and buildings in the vicinity. Have several "perc" tests made prior to buying so you will know there is adequate drainage.

3) Easements. Research the rights and privileges you may have to someone else's land, and they to yours. This is necessary for future roads, and for power and telephone lines. If someone else has an easement to your land, you will want to avoid planting your perennials or putting up a shed for the cows on that portion of your land.

4) Utilities. If you're far from civilization, will the power company come to you? Occasionally a company will refuse to install electricity unless you pay an exorbitant amount to bring it up your mountain or over the river.

5) Mineral Rights. There may be coal, gypsum, oil, or even gold on your land. Seemingly worthless land can yield surprises — surprises you want to be able to cash in on. There may be government restrictions regarding such land; find out from your town hall or local land assessor. Know your rights ahead of time.

6) Timber Rights. Usually this is not a problem area, yet if your land is heavily planted with trees, find out if there is a timber contract already in existence. A previous owner may have leased out rights to a logging company. If so, when does the contract expire? How much can the logging company take each year and for how long? To what condition must the land be restored after each harvest?

Self-protection is the key to successful land investments. Your lawyer and real estate broker can help protect you — but remember that even after paying earnest money (but only into an escrow account), your final purchase should be contingent on written statements covering the six items above. And, it's vital that you insist on a title search so you'll be aware of any encumbrances on the land. The title search will also unearth whether or not the owner really owns the land and if there's an underlying mortgage on the property, as well as if there are restrictions on access to minerals, water, or timber.

Finally, take time to study the area. If it is in a community, talk to other neighbors and residents. Find out the advantages and disadvantages of owning land there. All the information you gather will help you make a sound land decision that's best for you—not for the seller.

PART FOUR

Real Estate on Wall Street

When you hear the phrase "investing in real estate," you may immediately think of buying a house or condominium, or perhaps even purchasing an acre or two on which eventually to build your dream home. Those are the ways most Americans make money or build equity in the world of property.

Yet, there are other less traditional routes you can take that are just as sound and profitable—and you can get started with as little as $1,000.

In this section we will show you exactly how to earn high returns by investing in stocks, mutual funds, limited partnerships, and other real estate-related vehicles. You will learn how to earn 6.4 to 10.5 percent by owning shares in a real estate investment trust (REIT); or up to 15% if you purchase someone else's second mortgage. Then there are Ginnie Maes and other mortgage-backed securities, where not only are the yields high, but the securities are actually backed by agencies of the federal government.

Believe it or not, these and other Wall Street-type investments are available to the savvy real estate investor for much less than the cost of a split-level ranch or a colonial house.

16 Real Estate Investment Trusts

If you've been reluctant to dip your toe into the vast real estate pool, or if you want to enjoy the potential profits of commercial property but can't afford the price of an office building or an apartment house, then there is a sound, simple solution: real estate investment trusts. REITs, as they're often called, take the decision-making and hassle of owning real estate out of your hands and place it directly into those of a professional. Simple in concept, a well-run REIT can give you a high return on your investment. Let's see how they work and then set up some guidelines for selecting the best in the field.

REITs are rather like mutual funds—they pool together investors' dollars in order to purchase a portfolio of properties, mortgages, or both. These corporations are run by a professional management team, generally in conjunction with a shareholder-elected board of trustees. Their shares trade on the major stock exchanges as well as over the counter (*unlike* mutual funds, where units are sold directly by the fund or through brokers). The price of one share in a REIT can be as little as $15. Plan on a minimum of 100 shares to make it a worthwhile investment. As an investor who buys shares in the trust, you receive income on a regular basis.

REITS were initially established by Congress in 1960 in order to enable small investors to participate and benefit from commercial real estate without the problems and headaches associated with direct ownership. During the early 1970s these REITs took a huge beating due to poor-quality loans, rising interest rates, and an overbuilt commercial market. Shareholders across the nation lost over three billion dollars.

The picture today, however, is entirely different. There are close to 125 REITs being sold with total assets hovering around the 17-

77

billion-dollar mark. Why the turnaround? Managers learned their lesson—and today are far more careful about issuing loans and taking on too much debt. New federal guidelines control the amount of debt any one REIT can assume and thus protect the individual investor. In addition, REITs have increased in popularity due to the 1986 Tax Reform Act, and have become an appealing alternative to RELPs (real estate limited partnerships), many of which were virtually eliminated by the bill (see Chapter 17). One key advantage REITs have over RELPs is that they trade just like stocks over the various exchanges. RELPs, which are sold as units in a partnership, do not (unless they are Master Limited Partnerships in real estate, which are discussed in Chapter 18), and are therefore less liquid than REITs.

The primary advantage of REITs, however, is their high safety factor, which appeals to conservative investors. REITs are required by law to keep at least 75 percent of their assets in actual real estate investments, thus curbing any short-term speculation. (The remainder of the fund—no more than 25 percent—is kept in cash or highly liquid cash equivalents, such as U.S. government securities; this enables the fund to move quickly when good investment opportunities come along.) In addition, REITs must distribute or pass on 95 percent of their income to shareholders, thereby limiting the portion of the fund that can be soaked up by administrative costs.

Types of REITs

There are three basic types of REITs:

1) Equity REITs own portfolios of actual property, such as office buildings, shopping centers, malls, nursing homes, apartment buildings, etc. The REIT then earns income from two sources: from tenants' rents and from buying and selling properties. In 1986, equity REITs appreciated 12.6 percent.

Within this category, there is a special REIT you should be aware of. Known as a "single-property" REIT, it is set up to finance just one piece of property, such as a stadium. Then, although the trust retains ownership, the property is generally leased back to its original owners.

2) Mortgage REITs have their entire portfolios invested either in mortgages or construction loans, rather than actual property. Consequently they are considerably higher in risk than their equity counterparts, as they must often face loan defaults and interest fluctuations. In 1986, these REITs appreciated 6.4 percent.

According to Michael Dunbar, president of the National Association of Real Estate Investment Trusts, the mortgage variety is becoming increasingly safe, with managers exercising greater care regarding loans. In addition, such REITs are better protected from sharp changes in interest rates than in the past by the growing prevalence of flexible rate mortgages.

3) Hybrid REITs combine the two—their portfolios consist of both equity and mortgage REITs. They, too, appreciated 6.4 percent in 1986. Sometimes a REIT will be launched as a mortgage-based enterprise and then, over time, be turned into an equity REIT, or vice versa. Perhaps the best known example of a hybrid REIT is Rockefeller Center in New York City, which began as a mortgage REIT with a $1.3 billion investment and is scheduled to convert into an equity REIT in the year 2000.

Whether you decide to buy an equity, mortgage, or hybrid REIT, it will be either a self-liquidating or a perpetual-life trust.

Self-liquidating REITs have a predetermined length: They last for a certain number of years (many are 10 to 14 years, for example) and then are liquidated. When this happens, the profits are passed on to the shareholders. These REITs are also known as FREITs (Finite REITs) and can be compared in some ways to a bond: they trade closer to their value as the end approaches. In other words, the guaranteed liquidation date tends to boost share prices because the market takes into consideration the big cash payoff at the end.

Perpetual-life REITs are open-ended, and therefore the management can continually buy and sell property.

Selecting REITs

There are a number of criteria for picking out the best-performing REITs. Talk to your broker, of course, and read each annual report and prospectus to find out about the following things:

- **Diversification.** A REIT portfolio limited either to one particular type of real estate (office buildings, for example) or to one geographical area is riskier than a diversified REIT.

- **Quality.** Select a REIT whose property is already leased or rented. Half-full buildings spell trouble. In some areas of the country, office space is currently overbuilt, and REITs heavily focused on these areas are reporting lower profits.

- **Debt.** Find out about short-term debt. In the 1970s, many REITs faced severe financial problems because they were heavily leveraged. To protect your investment, select a REIT that is not heavily leveraged—in other words, one that doesn't owe significantly more than it has in assets. This is known as the debt-to-equity ratio, which should not be higher than 1:1. (In the mid-1970s the debt-to-equity ratio was more like 4:1.)

- **Management.** Read all available literature on the REIT you are considering to determine the management's qualifications. Look for at least ten years' experience in the real estate field.

- **Cash Flow.** Profits should be derived from ongoing operations—such as rental income or mortgage interest—rather than from the sale of properties. The latter serve only to increase cash flow on a one-time basis.

- **Dividend Growth.** Invest only in a REIT that has posted continual dividend growth. And make certain these dividends are being paid from earnings only, and not from the sale of property. REIT of America, for example, has been a consistent dividend payer.

- **Track Record.** Find out how long the trust has been in business; avoid those only a year or two old, since they have no documented history.

- **Non-Performing Loans.** A REIT must reveal the percentage of loans in default or not earning interest. Check the figures carefully with your accountant or stockbroker.

Tax Implications of REITs

REITs must distribute at least 95 percent of their net earnings to shareholders. In exchange for doing so they receive a tax break: Income and capital gains are exempt from corporate taxation. This, of course, tends to result in high dividends for shareholders. Consequently, REITs usually have higher yields than corporate stocks, which do not have such a tax break.

Mortgage REITs generally pay out a higher dividend than their equity counterparts. Yet, when an equity REIT sells property at a profit, the trust will then distribute the gains to shareholders. Hybrids pay out both dividends and capital gains.

REITs		
Company	**Price**	**Yield**
Bank America Realty	$31	7.7%
EQK Realty	16	10.5
HRE Properties	27	8.3
Lomas Mortgage	27	8.9
Mortgage & Realty Trust	21	8.7
Property Capital Trust	26	6.4
Rockefeller Center Properties	22	7.9
Wells Fargo Mortgage	23	8.6

(All prices as of 3/2/87)

Investment Advice

Generally speaking, equity REITs with substantially diversified holdings of commercial real estate offer more long-term growth potential as well as better protection against inflation than do mortgage REITs. The overabundance of office buildings at this time indicates that investors should select REITs that concentrate on shopping centers, nursing homes, and apartment buildings.

BECOME AN EXPERT

Ask your stockbroker for a list of REITs which you can contact for a copy of their annual report or prospectus. In addition, the following sources will provide you with valuable material:

- Audit Investments Inc. (publishes *Realty Stock Review*, a bi-monthly newsletter analyzing 100 different REITs) 136 Summit Avenue Montvale, NJ 07645 201-358-2735

- National Association of REITs 1101 17th Street, N.W. Washington, DC 20036 202-285-8717

- Value Line, Inc. (publishes
  an *Investment Survey*
  ranking REITs for timeliness
  and safety)
  711 Third Avenue
  New York, NY 10017
  212-687-3965

REAL ESTATE INVESTMENT TRUSTS

For Whom

- Those who want to participate indirectly in commercial real estate

- Those who can afford to make a moderately risky investment

Where to Purchase

- Through your stockbroker

Minimum

- Price of one share (as little as $15)

- Suggested minimum: 100 shares

Safety Factor

- Equity REITs are less risky than mortgage REITs (although mortgage REITs generally pay a higher dividend)

Advantages

- Dividend income

- High liquidity—shares trade on stock exchanges or OTC

- Potential price appreciation

- Way for smaller investor to participate in real estate

Disadvantages

- Price of shares subject to market risk

- Shares could drop in price

17 Real Estate Limited Partnerships

For years now, Congress has been cracking down on tax shelters, trying to tighten the noose around loopholes that allow investments geared toward generating tax losses rather than income.

The 1986 Tax Reform Act sharply curtailed a number of tax shelters, virtually knocking out those centered around "passive" activity—that is, investments in which the investor does not actively participate in the operation of the business. Included in the Congressional noose were real estate limited partnerships, or RELPs.

A limited partnership is an organization consisting of a general partner, who manages the program, and limited partners, who invest money in the program but have "limited" liability (that is, they can not lose more than their dollar contribution). The limited partners are passive investors and are not involved in the day-to-day business. All the limited partners share any benefits, such as cash distributions, capital gains or losses, and tax breaks, on a pro-rata basis.

Like REITs, RELPs invest in commercial properties and/or mortgages. But the corporate structure of RELPs is very different. The partnership is run by one or more general partners (in REITs a shareholder-elected Board of Trustees works in conjunction with a management team) and units are sold directly to investors. They do *not* trade on the exchanges, as REITs do, unless they are Master Limited Partnerships (see Chapter 18).

Units in a limited partnership are sold through stockbrokers, broker-dealers, and sometimes directly by syndicators, the people who organize and market the deal. You must meet certain financial requirements in order to participate: For example, you might need $50,000 in income and another $50,000 in net worth (excluding your car and house) for a standard $5,000 investment. The amount required is spelled out in the prospectus.

Public limited partnerships are registered with the Securities & Exchange Commission (SEC). Private limited partnerships, geared to the wealthy, are usually not registered with the SEC, and have higher minimums, usually $20,000 or more.

Due to tax reform, "phantom" (or "paper") losses in RELPs can no longer be used to offset income from your salary or from stocks and bonds. (These passive deductions, however, are not entirely useless. They can be used to offset income from other passive investments, currently or in the future.)

Make sure you have a reliable accountant who can determine if passive losses from one RELP can be offset by passive income from another limited partnership. To avoid this dilemma, look instead to income-producing programs such as REITs or MLPs, or to actively managing rental property, all of which are described in this book.

Income-Producing RELPs

Since the 1986 Tax Reform Act axed the heavily leveraged real estate limited partnerships, syndicators are now emphasizing income-producing programs, in which the partnership buys real estate primarily for cash, and *not* via mortgages or borrowed funds. These investments are sometimes called "all-cash" RELPs. Minimum investment ranges from $1,000 to $5,000. In these programs, a syndicator or general partner uses investors' money to buy or build office buildings, apartments, shopping malls, restaurants, day care centers, and other commercial properties.

Income for the partnership comes from rents. When taxes and expenses (including the general partner's share) are subtracted from this rental income, the remainder goes to you, the investor, as a limited partner. Generally, limited partners receive an initial "preferred" distribution: As rents are collected, a certain amount is distributed to the limited partners *before* the general partner begins to collect his percentage. Then, after the limited partners have received the specified amount, all further income is distributed *after* the general partner's share has been deducted. After a given number of years, usually five to ten, the partnership sells the properties and passes on the proceeds, known as appreciation, to the investors.

Income-producing RELPs should be designed to yield in excess of

10 percent annually over their lifetime—including annual cash payouts from rental income as well as eventual property appreciation. They are relatively safe because the partnership is not leveraged. In other words it borrows very little money, and so is not saddled with high interest payments.

SELECTING AN ALL-CASH RELP

- Read the prospectus to determine how successful previous offerings by the same syndicator were.

- Find out how much of your money actually goes toward buying property.

- How much does the general partner take out for salaries and administrative expenses? How much are brokerage fees? These two combined should never be more than 30 percent.

- Have your lawyer or accountant review the prospectus and advise you regarding the financial soundness of the program.

The Risks Involved

All-cash RELPs are not totally free from risk, however, despite such claims by many of the syndicators. These are the key items to watch out for: First of all, overbuilding in certain areas of the country has pushed up vacancy rates in office buildings and consequently pushed down rental income. Second, partnerships tend to be illiquid: If you want out before the end, you have to sell in a secondary market (if there is one), and often you'll wind up selling at a loss. And finally, new unoccupied buildings are riskier than those already rented.

BECOME AN EXPERT

Contact the following sponsors of all-cash RELPs for a prospectus:

- Aetna Real Estate Assoc./
  E.F. Hutton
  (Contact any office)

- Angeles Group
  Los Angeles, CA
  800-421-4374

- Realty Income Corp.
  Escondito, CA
  800-854-1967

- T. Rowe Price
  Baltimore, MD
  800-638-5660

Two excellent monthly newsletters rate partnerships and provide details on risk level, fees, and type of programs being sold:

- *The Partnership Record*
  ($250/year)
  Southport Advisors
  P.O. Box 682
  Southport, CT 06490
  203-254-0510

- *Stanger Register*
  ($225/year)
  1129 Broad St.
  Shrewsbury, NJ 07701
  201-389-3600

Mini-Storage RELPs

Here's an income-producing limited partnership that is inexpensive to invest in and which over the past several years has offered excellent returns, sometimes as high as 20 percent. Mini-storage RELPs are limited partnerships that own small warehouses. Units are available from stockbrokers, with minimums ranging from $1,000 to $2,500.

Mini-warehouses rent out small storage areas to individuals and small businesses. Very few services are provided. Renters move their things in and out, so each warehouse really needs only one or two employees to manage the facility, plus a maintenance or custodial person. Low labor costs are one reason these investments have yielded high returns. Rents are collected monthly. Once the units are rented, it is generally easy to institute modest rental increases.

When the mini-storage movement began in the early 1960s, it consisted primarily of "mom-and-pop" operations in the South and Southwest. Recently, however, the trend has been toward large centrally-operated chains, such as Public Storage, which runs 475 warehouses in over 30 states.

Chains have also led to overbuilding in certain areas (Houston, Dallas, and Denver, for example). Nevertheless, analysts believe yields to investors of between 10 and 15 percent are not out of the question in most parts of the country. These returns are derived from rental income distribution and capital appreciation when the partnership is liquidated (most mini-storage RELPs are designed to last ten years; some last five).

Since mini-storage partnerships were never designed to provide tax breaks, they were not hit by the 1986 Tax Reform Act. They carry very little debt since the facilities are generally purchased or constructed with cash from the partnership.

When evaluating a mini-storage investment:

- Find out the location of the majority of warehouses; avoid programs centered in overbuilt areas.

- Ask if the existing properties have been able to raise their rents; this is an indication of strength.

- Look for a solid program — one in which the occupancy rate is likely to reach 90 percent within the first year.

- In a new program, make certain the "front-end" costs (see page 93), including the general partner's fees and profits, do not exceed 30 percent.

BECOME AN EXPERT

Contact these mini-storage RELPs for further information:

- Public Storage, Inc.
  Pasadena, CA
  800-421-2856

- Balcor Company
  Chicago, IL
  312-677-2900

- DSI Properties
  Long Beach, CA
  213-599-2425

- Storage Equities, Inc.
  Glendale, CA
  818-244-9841

The mini-storage trade association will also provide material:

- Self-Service Storage Association
  P.O. Box 110
  Eureka Springs, AR 72632
  501-253-7701

Selling Your RELP

General partners typically close out a RELP in between eight and ten years; many go right on to establish new limited partnerships. When the properties are sold, the money received is distributed to the investors, who then must pay tax on the gain.

If you must sell your investment in a RELP before the partnership is dissolved, you will need to find what is known as a "secondary" market (such as a stockbroker or syndicator) through which to sell it.

There are also specialized services that make a market in secondary RELPs—such as the *National Partnership Exchange* (NAPEX), in St. Petersburg, Florida (800-356-2739), a computerized matching service that posts listings of limited partnerships for sale. NAPEX members have seven days in which to bid on offerings; the seller then has the right to accept or reject the bid. (You can also use NAPEX as a way to buy shares of RELPs at a discount.)

Another source is the *Liquidity Fund Investment*, in Emeryville, CA (800-227-4688 or 415-652-1462). This fund buys out partnership interests and then repackages them into new partnerships. The firm looks for SEC-registered limited partnerships and shuns highly leveraged deals set up as tax shelters. If you go this route, you will have to sell your units at a substantial discount, perhaps as much as 35 percent. This should indicate to you the importance of considering RELP investments for the long term only.

Other sources for selling RELPs include:

- MacKenzie Securities   800-854-8357
  Oakland, CA   415-362-1018

- Oppenheimer & Biegelow Management   800-431-7811
  New York, NY   212-599-0697

- Partnership Securities Exchange   415-763-5555
  Oakland, CA

18 Master Limited Partnerships

This hybrid investment trades like a stock, provides income like a bond, and offers a handful of important tax breaks. Master limited partnerships (MLPs) are companies held in partnership form in which stock has been exchanged for units of the partnership. The first ones appeared on the scene in the early 1980s in the oil and gas industry, and now, given a boost by the 1986 Tax Reform Act, have just started to move into the real estate field. Currently they are averaging a 10-percent return.

MLPs are often compared to RELPs, and in one way they are very much like them: All income and losses flow directly to the limited partners (the investors). Yet, MLPs differ from RELPs in one important way: They trade on the stock exchange and therefore are much more liquid then RELPs. Their units can be sold at any time at the going market rate.

There's also an important distinction in the way they are structured. MLPs can be formed in two ways: either by gathering together a number of small partnerships and putting them under one "master" umbrella, or by structuring the partnership as an MLP from the outset. The new tax law makes them particularly popular because an MLP, unlike a corporation, is *not* a taxable entity, and therefore does not pay federal tax at the partnership or company level.

Here is how corporate taxation works: A corporation such as Exxon or IBM must pay federal tax on its profits. But part of these profits are distributed to shareholders (in the form of dividends), and shareholders themselves must then pay taxes on this income. In effect, this is double taxation: once at the corporate level and once at the investor level. But investors in an MLP only pay tax once, on distributions; the partnership itself pays no federal tax. (Because of this discrepancy an increasing number of corporations are seriously considering the possible advantages of disincorporating.)

Many real estate MLPs stem from corporations with large real estate assets—restaurants, hotels, and nursing homes. An outstanding example of a recent MLP was the Burger King deal. A subsidiary of Pillsbury, this number-two fast food chain sold off 128 of its Burger King sites to the public. The new entity, called Burger King Investors Master Limited Partnership, received the deeds and leases to the 128 Burger King restaurants. Units were issued at $20 apiece, with an initial yield of 9.4 percent.

Among the large real estate firms that have gone or are in the process of going the MLP route are Standard-Pacific Corporation, Newhall Land & Farming Company, N.V. Homes, Universal Development Corporation, and Commonwealth Mortgage of America. Standard-Pacific's decision was based on its tax situation. This corporation's 1985 tax bill was a whopping 12 million dollars, yet as an MLP it would pay no taxes and have that much more cash to either distribute to investors or plow back into the company.

Tax Advantages

Depending upon the deal, the investors/limited partners in an MLP may receive some tax-sheltered cash distributions, known as "return of capital." This means that a portion of the partnership's income may be free from current taxation because it is offset by paper tax deductions generated by depreciation. For example, assume an annual net income (after expenses) of $2,000 and a yearly depreciation of $800. The depreciation can be deducted from the $2,000 profit, thereby reducing the current taxable income to $1,200 and leaving a current tax-sheltered "return of capital" of $800. Although the entire $2,000 is distributed to the limited partners, they pay current taxes *only* on that portion which is not offset by depreciation. In the case of Burger King, for example, 60 percent of the payout is taxable, while 40 percent is a tax-sheltered return of capital.

You can find out about current MLPs from your stockbroker or financial advisor. Be sure to avoid MLPs that are last-minute efforts to save a failing company.

EXAMPLES OF MLPs

Company	Price	Yield
Burger King Investors	$20	9.4%
EQK Greenacres	11	9.9
Newhall Investment Properties	11	5.6
UDC-Universal Development	25	8.8
UMB Equities	1½	nil

(All prices as of 3/2/87)

---

19 Investing in Mortgages

For the investor interested in putting money into mortgages, rather than actual properties, there are two common alternatives: mortgage loan partnerships and second mortgages.

Mortgage Loan Partnerships

Mortgage loan partnerships are limited partnerships which lend money invested by individuals to developers and other real estate professionals to build properties. The borrowers commit to pay the partnership a fixed rate of interest on the mortgage loan, and often participation in future profits (such as rental income or appreciation in the value of the real estate involved) as well.

Units in the partnership are sold by stockbrokers, financial planners, and sometimes directly by the syndicators—those who are putting the deal together. This investment provides a steady stream of fixed income to the investor and usually pays higher rates than such instruments as CDs, money market funds, and T-Bills. Currently they range from 6 to 18 percent, depending upon the interest rate the partnership charges the buyers. The higher the rate, the riskier the investment.

There are approximately 35 public mortgage loan partnerships available. A partial list is given on page 94. The minimum investment is $1,000, although most require $2,000 to $2,500. Public partnerships are registered with the Securities & Exchange Commission (SEC) and therefore must disclose certain financial details about their company; this protects the investor.

How They Work

Mortgage loan partnerships are structured as limited partnerships and therefore are quite different from a traditional corporation. In a limited partnership, a syndicator puts the deal together and then manages it. He's known as the general partner. He sells units (not shares on a stock exchange) to hundreds of investors, who are called limited partners; they are the ones who put up most of the money. The general partner may also put in money, although he is not required to in most cases; this varies from deal to deal.

A mortgage loan partnership, unlike an equity REIT (see Chapter 16), does *not* own property; it only lends money. As borrowers pay back their mortgages to the partnership, the interest and principal are passed on to the investors/limited partners (after the general partner's share is deducted), generally in quarterly payments. The average partnership matures in twelve years.

In a mortgage loan partnership, the mortgaged property must either be sold or appraised when the loan comes due. The borrower then pays the partnership a previously agreed-upon percentage of any increase in the value of the property. This profit in turn is distributed proportionately to the investors. The return can vary, depending upon the success of the deal. For example, a borrower might agree to pay 8 percent interest on a mortgage and 24 percent of any increase in cash flow from rents and appreciation of mortgaged property. In this setup the limited partners would benefit during inflationary periods, when rents and property values tend to rise.

The Risk Involved

If a borrower defaults on payments, investors could, of course, lose money. And—as is true with all investments that pay a fixed or set rate of return—when interest rates go up, the value of already-existing units goes down. This is because newer units pay higher rates, which in turn undermines the value of the older ones.

In most mortgage loan partnerships there's another minus: You don't know precisely where your money is going to be invested ahead of time because the money is raised first and then the developer/borrowers are brought into the situation. This means you're relying totally on the cleverness and wisdom of the general partner to find sound developers—so it's *extremely* important to check the general partner's track record. If he's been setting up tax shelters in cattle or in Broadway plays, it's quite unlikely he's a real estate expert, too.

Getting out of a mortgage loan partnership may present problems, as well. If you want to sell your units before the partnership is dissolved, you may not find a buyer. Therefore, this investment is not suggested for those who may need to tap their money on short notice. If you're seeking a more liquid investment, turn to Chapter 18, on Master Limited Partnerships.

Selecting a Mortgage Loan Partnership

Check the list below and talk to your broker or accountant. Read all promotional literature and the prospectus. The latter can be dreary reading, but you must look for certain facts. Read to find out about the partnership's objectives, how it plans to use the proceeds, what the risk levels are, and how taxes will be handled.

It's also important to know what the general partner's previous experience has been and how much of the fund goes to "front-end" costs. These charges—which include sales commission, administrative costs, and an "acquisition fee" to the general partner—should be no more than 30 percent maximum. All of this will be spelled out for you in the partnership's prospectus, in a "Use of Proceeds" table.

Ask about the types of loans being made. The most common and also the most conservative are first mortgages. The safest of all mortgage loan partnerships are those that make government guaranteed loans—in multi-family housing or special projects, for example. Second in safety are mortgages that carry some type of insurance.

If you're less concerned about risk and more interested in high returns, look for a partnership that makes construction loans or takes second mortgages. These are not government-backed.

A mortgage loan partnership's prospectus should also discuss the loan-to-value ratio. This is one of the best ways to assess the risk quotient. If the property costs a half-million dollars, you don't want to lend the purchaser the full half-million. You want some of the purchaser's money involved so that if the property falls in value, *his* money is lost too, not just the mortgage money your partnership has lent to the developer.

The loan-to-value ratio tells how much the developer should put up. For conservative investors it should be no more than 65 percent. The more money the owner has in the property, the less risk to the partnership—but also the less income you will receive as a lender.

If a borrower does not make his payments and subsequently defaults, the limited partnership might end up owning the property involved. That's why the loan-to-value ratio is so crucial: You want property than can be sold at a high enough price to cover the loan.

For further information, contact the following Mortgage Loan Partnership sponsors:

- Aetna/E.F. Hutton
  New York, NY
  212-742-5000

- Balcor Co.
  Chicago, IL
  312-677-2900

- Consolidated Capital Equities Corp.
  Emeryville, CA
  415-652-7171

- JMB Realty Corp.
  Chicago, IL
  312-440-4800

- Oxford National
  Bethesda, MD
  301-654-3100

- Shearson/Lehman
  New York, NY
  212-298-2000

- VMS Realty
  Chicago, IL
  312-399-8700

Second Mortgages

If you've got time and some extra cash, you can often achieve impressive results by investing in or financing second mortgages. There are two basic ways to do this: One is to buy an existing second mortgage at a discount—a mortgage that's already been made by a homeowner to a home buyer as explained below; or, you can finance the second mortgage yourself.

Discounted Second Mortgages

Second mortgages are often made by a homeowner to the buyer of his house if the buyer's down payment and first mortgage are not quite enough to buy the house. In most cases, the borrower makes monthly payments, but only on the interest, because a second mortgage is usually a short-term balloon loan—typically five years, but with a payment schedule based on 30 years. The large balloon payment comes due at the end of the fifth year.

Interest rates on second mortgages tend to be $1\frac{1}{2}$ to $2\frac{1}{2}$ percentage points above first mortgages. Here's where you, the investor, come in: If for various reasons, the seller (or grantor of the second mortgage) wants to free up his cash before the balloon payment is due, he can sell his second mortgage at a discount to an investor such as yourself. For example, the seller could grant the buyer a second mortgage for $10,000 at 12 percent. The loan period is three years, but the seller unexpectedly needs cash and prefers not to wait that long for his balloon payment of the principal. You offer to buy the seller's second mortgage note at a discount, say for $8,500. This will in turn provide you with a lump sum payment of $10,000 in three years and interest payments along the way.

There are several types of second mortgage holders willing to sell to investors. One is the seller who was forced to take a second mortgage during a poor economic climate in order to sell his house. Another is the seller who moves or is transferred far away from the locale of the transaction involved and does not want to be responsible for continuous long-distance collection. A third type is someone who needs immediate cash; a fourth is a home improvement contractor who often lends money to his clients and then sells these notes below their face value to other lenders.

In buying a second mortgage at a discount, you in essence become the bank, offering immediate cash in return for collecting more cash over the long run. The key point, of course, is never to buy a mortgage at its original dollar amount. The rule of thumb is to pay five percent less than face value for each year left on the loan.

If it's easier on your pocketbook, you can buy just a part of a mortgage—two year's worth, for instance. Sellers often find this appealing because it means they will still receive some steady income.

Selecting a Second Mortgage

Prior to investing in a second mortgage, you must do some homework:

- What is the credit rating of the owner? Can he or she meet both first and second mortgage payments?

- What is the resale value of the property? Will it cover the outstanding loans? The loan-to-value ratio should be in the neighborhood of 2:3.

- If you're financing a second mortgage directly, what is the amount of equity the owner has in the property? In the event of a foreclosure you want to be certain it's sufficient to cover not only the first and second loans but also any tax lien placed on the property. The recommended minimum is 20 percent. Keep in mind that in a foreclosure, the real estate taxes come first, then the first mortgage, and finally you.

- Visit the property. Would you want to own it? If it's in a poor neighborhood where values may decline, either skip it, or, if you're the one doing the financing, charge more for assuming this extra risk.

- Get the property appraised.

Financing and investing in second mortgages are complicated transactions and should not be left to amateurs. Always have a real estate lawyer review all the pertinent documents.

WHERE TO FIND SECOND MORTGAGES

- Advertise in your local paper or firm's newsletter.
- List yourself with local realtors. Many maintain names of those willing to invest in second mortgages.
- Contact a mortgage broker.
- Talk to building contractors and those who do remodeling.

20 Real Estate Stocks and Mutual Funds

The stock market provides several interesting avenues to investing in real estate, whether you invest directly in real estate stocks or indirectly, through a mutual fund.

Real Estate Stocks

Fueled by low interest rates, an active housing market, and aging baby boomers who need more space, a number of these stocks are currently of interest. Keep in mind, however, that they are never continually in favor. Before building a housing portfolio, review the economics of each individual stock. Read the company's annual report and any research materials your stockbroker can provide, as well as reports published by Value Line Investment Survey and Standard & Poor's.

A partial list of stocks analyzed by Value Line is given below. In addition, you may want to consider stocks of home builders and suppliers.

COMPANY	EXCHANGE	PRICE	YIELD
AMREP Corp. 10 Columbus Circle New York, NY 10019 212-541-7300	NYSE:AXR	$15	nil
Bay Financial 200 State St. Boston, MA 02019 617-439-6046	NYSE:BAY	$26½	.7%

The Deltona Corp. 3250 S.W. Third Ave. Miami, FL 33129 305-854-1111	NYSE:DLT	$ 6	nil
Fairfield Communities 2800 Cantrell Rd. Little Rock, AK 72202 501-664-6000	NYSE:FCI	$ 7	nil
Horizon Corp. 16838 E. Palisades Blvd. Fountain Hills, AZ 85268 602-837-1685	NYSE:HZN	$ 5	nil
The Koger Co. 3986 Boulevard Center Dr. Jacksonville, FL 32207 904-396-4817	ASE:KGR	$30	8.0%
Koger Properties 3986 Boulevard Center Dr. Jacksonville, FL 32207 904-396-4811	NYSE:KOG	$31	8.4%
Newall Land & Farming Co. 23823 Valencia Blvd. Valencia, CA 91355 802-255-4000	NYSE:NHL	$37	2.1%
Radice Corp. 600 Corporate Dr. Ft. Lauderdale, FL 33334 305-493-5003	NYSE:RI	$10	nil
Rouse Co. Rouse Co. Bldg. Columbia, MD 21044 301-992-6000	OTC:ROUS	$34	1.8%
Vornado, Inc. 174 Passaic St. Garfield, NJ 07026 201-773-4000	NYSE:VNO	$81	nil

Del E. Webb Corp.   NYSE:WBB $20   1.0%
3800 North Central Ave.
Phoenix, AZ 85012
602-264-8011

(All prices as of 3/2/87)

Mutual Funds

A real estate mutual fund enables even the smallest investor to participate in real estate. A mutual fund is an investment company that buys and sells stocks and bonds on behalf of individual investors. The fund pools together money from many people, each with varying amounts to invest. Professional portfolio managers use this money to purchase a variety of stocks and bonds—in this case, those investing in real estate—to meet the fund's stated objective. When the fund earns money, it distributes earnings to the shareholders.

If you don't have the time or inclination to participate in real estate directly, you can turn to one of the two professionally managed real estate mutual funds instead.

The National Real Estate Stock Fund, run by the National Securities & Research Corporation of New York, invests shareholders' money in the stocks of 30 companies, all of which are involved in some form of real estate—REITs, homebuilding companies, developers, finance companies, etc. (Such diversity spreads out the risk so that difficulties or declining prices in any one company will not drag down the fund's total performance record.) The minimum investment in the National Real Estate Stock Fund is $500. There is a 7.7-percent sales charge for investments under $25,000. For a copy of the prospectus, call 800-331-3420 (212-661-3000 in New York).

In October 1986, Fidelity Management & Research Company started its *Fidelity Real Estate Portfolio*, which invests in real estate stocks and bonds. This fund, which is both growth- and income-oriented, has an initial minimum investment requirement of $2,500. The sales charge is two percent. For a copy of the prospectus, call 800-544-6666.

21 | Vulture Funds

The commercial real estate market is a mercurial one, and at times certain sections of the country are glutted with partially vacant office buildings, hotels, and in some cases, apartments. Today, Houston, Dallas, Denver, New Orleans, and Fort Lauderdale are overbuilt. Tomorrow it may be your area.

The glut has attracted a new type of syndicate specializing in so-called "distressed property." Managers of these syndicates comb areas in search of properties being unloaded by developers and lenders at reduced prices.

How Vulture Funds Work

"Vulture funds" are open to the public on a limited basis. Investors pool their money together and put it in the hands of a general partner who buys and sells various properties. Shares or units in the funds are sold to the public through stockbrokers and sponsors, with a required minimum investment of $2,500. The investors have no say-so in the portfolio's contents. Most funds are designed to last three to seven years; at the end of that time they will have sold all their properties, presumably at a profit.

If you decide to invest in a vulture fund, don't expect to see much income during the first years. In this turnaround period properties may be renovated, new tenants found, management changed. In its early years, the fund may also incur various losses, but once the properties start to make money again, investors start to receive periodic distributions. Then when a property is sold, additional proceeds are made. A portion of this payout is treated as a return of capital (see page 90) and therefore is free of current federal income tax (check with your accountant for details).

The vulture fund managers are of course counting on a turnaround in the currently distressed market. If and when that takes place, you could conceivably receive annual returns ranging from between 10 and 15 percent, or higher. If you believe that prices are at their lows, then that may be the right time to invest in a vulture fund. (Keep in mind, however, that if the market does *not* take a turn for the better, you may not make a profit, and even run the risk of losing your investment altogether.)

One reason for investor optimism in vulture funds is the new tax law. Real estate shelters have been hard hit by tax reform, and limited partnerships no longer offer as much tax incentive as they used to. This means that 1) overbuilding could decline because there will be fewer limited partnerships; and 2) there is a better resale market for existing commercial space because limited partnerships in *new* spaces have been axed for the most part.

The Risks Involved

The basic drawback is that vulture funds are often new (under two years old), lacking adequate track records. The only basis for judgment is how well the syndicator has done in the past. Be sure to ask the general partner for information concerning previous real estate deals. You should also ask your broker about the general partner's reputation and background.

Keep in mind that buildings may need repairs, and cash flow may be slow for the first years of the fund. The syndicate may also own poor-quality property that is incapable of being turned around. If this is the case the new tax law makes such tax losses less valuable than in the past. You will most likely *not* be able to currently write off a loss against ordinary income—your salary, for example. Check with your accountant as to how to handle such losses.

To reduce their risks, now that tax losses are not always an appealing sales point, some vulture funds are buying properties with cash up front.

Selecting a Vulture Fund

Since the risks here are exceptionally high, it's important to know the facts. Read the fund's prospectus and talk to your accountant about management's predictions for both rental increases and the fund's potential return. Beware of projects that are based primarily on inflation rather than income. How long does the sponsor anticipate the turnaround time to be? What if it takes longer? Can he sustain an extension or will he have to sell the properties? How much of your investment actually goes into real estate? (Typically up to 30 percent goes for fees and commissions.) General partners usually take a percentage (often as much as 45 percent) of the cash flow and capital gains. However, most don't collect until after the investors have received their preferred return (see page 84). Check out all the facts with a real estate expert before flying with the vultures.

BECOME AN EXPERT

For additional information, contact the following vulture funds:

- Angeles Opportunity
  Properties
  Los Angeles, CA
  800-421-4374

- August Financial Corp.
  Long Beach, CA
  213-424-5100

- Equity Resources Group
  Cambridge, MA
  617-876-4800

- The Liquidity Fund
  Emeryville, CA
  415-652-1462

- National Partnership
  Exchange
  St. Petersburg, FL
  800-356-2739

22 | Municipal Tax Sales

You can often make double-digit returns on tax sales investments in exchange for paying a property owner's delinquent real estate taxes. You can find such an opportunity at annual municipal tax sales.

Most municipalities throughout the country have annual tax sales, held in the form of auctions. They do this in order to collect unpaid real estate tax money needed to maintain their schools and fire or police departments. Although the procedures vary from place to place, the basics are the same, and notice is usually posted in several public places prior to the sale.

Investors are promised a stated interest rate if they pay the municipality someone else's delinquent real estate taxes: The delinquent homeowner must repay the back taxes, plus the stated interest, to the investor/lien-holder. The investor's insurance is his right to foreclose on the real estate if the owner never does repay him. The amount of back taxes an investor may have to pay on a given property can vary widely—from one hundred to several thousand dollars.

In this type of investment, you are counting on the fact that the property will bring more in a foreclosure sale than what you have paid in overdue taxes to the town. And in just about all cases that is what happens.

For example, a New Jersey investor recently paid approximately $9,000 in back taxes on a large piece of property. The annual interest rate was 18 percent. The owner has two years in which to repay the investor the taxes plus interest. If he fails to pay, the investor will foreclose on the property. (He will probably get far more than $9,000 should he have to foreclose and resell. And even if the investor doesn't foreclose, he will earn substantial interest on his investment—in this case, 18 percent.)

Tax sales are not to be confused with municipal auctions, where property is up on the block (see Chapter 5). At a tax sale you bid on the lien on the property, not on the property itself. These liens prevent the owners from selling their property. Once the overdue taxes are paid in full, however, the owner is free to sell.

At the Auction

Most states place a cap on the top interest rate property owners can be charged for late taxes. This figure ranges from 18 to 50 percent. (You can find out the top interest rate figure by calling your local tax collector.) The bidding at the auction begins at the highest possible rate, and the bidder willing to take the lowest rate wins the lien. If your bid is the winner, be prepared then and there to write a check (covering the back taxes owed on the property) to the municipality for the tax lien you've purchased. In return, you will receive a sales certificate which you must register with the county clerk. Should you fail to register and if there's another lien holder, that person could make a first claim in the event of a foreclosure sale.

After the tax sale, the property owner receives an extension for a stated period of time, during which he must pay you, the investor, the overdue taxes plus the stated interest. Failure to pay means you can start foreclosure proceedings. This grace period is set by state law and can be as little as six months, but is more often one to two years.

The Risks Involved

Although the rate you may receive can be high—18 to 50 percent—so are the risks. First of all, although most property owners wind up paying their back taxes, there is no guarantee that they will. Second, you do not know exactly when you will be repaid, although it should be within the lawfully stated time period. Third, your investment is not immediately liquid, like a stock, bond, REIT, or MLP. The only ways to get your money back are to be paid by the homeowner, or to foreclose on the property. Foreclosure sales are not pleasant and can be costly and time-consuming.

If you decide to invest in tax liens, protect your investment by visiting the property prior to bidding at the auction. You want to know it's not a toxic waste dump but rather something the owners would like to keep and/or that you could readily sell after a foreclosure, should that be necessary.

For further information, contact tax collectors in your area to get the dates of auctions as well as the top interest rate being paid.

23 Mortgage-Backed Securities

There are a number of mortgage-backed securities you can buy from your stockbroker or through a mutual fund, all of which offer competitive yields with relatively low risk. The first and still the most popular of these mortgage-backed securities are Ginnie Maes.

Ginnie Maes

"Ginnie Mae" stands for the Government National Mortgage Association (GNMA), a wholly-owned corporation of the federal government whose purpose is to stimulate housing by bringing investment money into the real estate market. GNMA was created in 1968 and is part of the Department of Housing & Urban Development. Ginnie Maes have the highest yields of all government-guaranteed securities, generally exceeding those of Treasury Bonds by up to two percentage points.

A Ginnie Mae is set in motion when a homebuyer takes out a mortgage; the house is pledged as collateral. A mortgage banker then pools this and other 30-year FHA- or VA-backed mortgages into packages or pools of mortgages worth one million dollars or more. Upon GNMA approval, $25,000 certificates are sold against these pools. The certificates are backed by the FHA- and VA-insured mortgages.

Homebuyers in the meantime make their monthly interest and principal payments to the bank. A share of these payments is passed through to the investors—those owning Ginnie Mae certificates. (This is where the term "pass through" comes from—both the mortgage principal and interest payments pass through to the investor from the banker.)

Ginnie Maes are particularly safe since they carry the "direct full faith and credit guarantee" of the U.S. government. (Others in the Mae family carry an indirect guarantee, as explained below.) This guarantee protects investors from default by homeowners in that it says that interest and principal will be paid whether or not homeowners pay back their lending institutions.

Ginnie Mae Mutual Funds

You need $25,000 to buy a Ginnie Mae certificate, but you can participate for far less by purchasing shares in a Ginnie Mae mutual fund. (See page 99 on how mutual funds work.) The fund, which invests in Ginnie Mae certificates, will send you a monthly check based upon the fund's earnings.

But, keep in mind that there are risks involved: Ginnie Maes do *not* guarantee the interest rate or the amount you will be paid, or precisely when you will receive it. Fund managers try to keep their yields as high as possible, but when interest rates fall, thousands of homeowners prepay their mortgages and refinance at lower rates. That means the mortgages in the pool are closed out early and the Ginnie Mae mutual fund manager is forced to reinvest the fund's money in new certificates which of course are issued at a lower rate. The value of your fund shares will fluctuate depending upon how rapidly homeowners pay back their mortgages and what rates are assigned to newly issued certificates.

Some funds are allowed to invest portions of their portfolios in other types of investments, such as Treasury issues which are equally safe. But others turn to somewhat riskier real estate-backed securities—Freddie Macs and Fannie Maes, or even non-guaranteed mortgages—to keep their yields high. The riskiest funds sell options against their portfolios to maintain higher yields.

Before investing in any mutual fund, read the prospectus to see precisely what securities it may buy and sell. If you're concerned with safety, stick to those with only Ginnie Maes and U.S. Treasury Bonds. The prospectus will also spell out details about check-writing privileges, sales fees, and dividend reinvestment procedures.

LEADING GNMA FUNDS   Yields*

- Colonial Government Mortgage Fund   7.37%
  Boston, MA
  617-426-3750
  800-225-2365

- Dreyfus GNMA Fund   8.90
  New York, NY
  212-715-6000
  800-645-6561

- Fidelity GNMA Portfolio   7.50
  Boston, MA
  617-570-7000
  800-544-6666

- John Hancock U.S. Government Guaranteed   7.99
  Boston, MA
  617-421-6000
  800-225-5291

- Lexington GNMA Income Fund   7.82
  Saddle Brook, NJ
  201-845-7300
  800-526-0056

- U.S.A.A. Income Fund   8.50
  San Antonio, TX
  512-498-8000
  800-531-8000

*Yields as of 3/2/87

Freddie Macs
and Fannie Maes

Ginnie Mae led the way for both Freddie Mac (the Federal Home Loan Mortgage Corporation) and Fannie Mae (the Federal National Mortgage Association), both of which issue mortgage-backed certificates similar to Ginnie Maes. The FHLMC and the FNMA invest in pools primarily consisting of "conventional" home mortgages rather than those insured by the FHA and the VA. Both Freddie and Fannie sell $25,000 certificates against these pools. Although the FHLMC and the FNMA are not officially part of the government, they have indirect government backing (both corporations are chartered by Congress) and are considered almost as high in safety as Ginnie Maes.

Just like Ginnie Maes, Freddie Macs and Fannie Maes pass on to investors monthly principal and interest payments made by homeowners on their mortgages.

Since Freddie Macs and Fannie Maes lack the direct government guarantee that Ginnie Maes carry, the added element of risk brings slightly higher yields. A number of Ginnie Mae mutual funds invest a percentage of their fund in Freddie Macs and Fannie Maes.

Collateralized
Mortgage Obligations

Also called CMOs, these are mortgage-backed bonds. They were introduced in 1983 by the Federal Home Loan Mortgage Corporation to address the key problem inherent in Ginnie Maes — that investors never know exactly how much they will receive each month or for how long. As explained above, this uncertainty is due to the fact that homeowners frequently pay off their mortgages early — to refinance at lower rates or because they move. This happens so frequently, in fact, that the average 30-year mortgage has a true life of only 12 years.

CMO bonds are AAA-rated — the highest rating possible — and are collateralized by mortgage-backed pass-through securities (Ginnie Maes, Freddie Macs, and Fannie Maes). They are usually available in $1,000, $5,000, and $25,000 units, although there are variations within brokerage firms.

The individual bonds are divided into four classes: A, B, C, and Z. Each class has a different interest rate and a different maturity date. Class A bonds have lower interest rates, shorter maturities, and higher safety than class Z. Classes A, B, and C pay semi-annual interest at a specified rate until the bonds are "retired" (paid off). At that point, having already received your interest payments, your initial dollar investment is returned to you. However, with Class Z, the longest CMO, investors get *all* principal and interest payments in one lump sum, when the bond matures.

It's important to note that with CMOs, as with all bonds, when interest rates decline issuers can—and commonly do—call in (or "retire") these bonds before their maturity date. (This allows them to issue new bonds at lower rates.) So, although investors in CMOs receive a steady, guaranteed rate of return each month, it is impossible to predict precisely when the bonds will be retired. But the degree of uncertainty is far less than with Ginnie Maes, Freddie Macs, and Fannie Maes.

CMO SAMPLER

Class	Yield	Maturity	Average Expected Life
A	7.74%	2/20/09	3.43 years
B	9.10%	8/20/09	7.81
C	9.55%	8/20/12	10.88
Z	10.64%	11/20/17	17.69

(Kidder, Peabody & Co.)

PART FIVE

Nuts and Bolts

24 Mortgages and Creative Financing

When buying your first house you are faced with the seemingly awesome chore of financing. Digging up the down payment alone—11 percent of the purchase price, on average—is no easy task. On a $140,000 house, for example, that is $15,400. On top of that you may have to pay an additional $2,000 to $4,000 for points, title insurance, and closing costs. Even if you've been stashing away every spare penny, you may not have it in your back pocket. Here are some proven and often overlooked ways to solve the problem.

Government Help. Mortgages insured by the Veterans Administration and the Federal Housing Administration are there to help those unable to make large down payments. You actually obtain the mortgage from a bank, but it is guaranteed or insured against default by the VA or FHA.

VA loans are available to eligible former members of the Armed

Forces and to the spouse of any veteran who was killed, is missing in action, or has been a prisoner of war for 90 days or longer. Interest rates are set by the VA, and are always lower than standard bank mortgages, usually by about one percent. The down payment on these mortgages is generally very low—and sometimes, none is required at all. The VA guarantees mortgages of up to 60 percent of the cost of a single-family home, to a maximum of $27,500. This guaranteed amount commonly serves as an acceptable base, on which banks construct VA mortgages for more substantial amounts (often up to $100,000). The amount backed by the VA usually provides sufficient security and incentive to the lending institution to provide non-guaranteed funding for the balance of the mortgage, despite a small cash down payment. Since it takes a fairly long time to process a VA loan, contact your local bank immediately for details

FHA loans are available to anyone who meets the criteria. Interest rates, set by the bank (not the FHA), are not necessarily lower than regular loans. Nonetheless, three points make FHA loans worth looking into: low down payment, a long maturity (up to 30 years), and the option for mortgage prepayment without penalty. Check with your local FHA office regarding eligibility and current regulations, which vary geographically. At the present time most FHA mortgages require *only* three to five percent down; however, the lending institution may require more, and generally insists that your monthly mortgage payments and any other fixed payments not exceed 33 percent of your gross income. In addition, the mortgage payment can only be 25 percent of your income.

The real appeal of both VA and FHA loans is not so much that interest rates are lower as that down payments can be smaller, and financial requirements are more lenient than with regular mortgages.

Retirement Money. Try tapping your profit-sharing plan at work, either by withdrawing or by borrowing the money (although employers may not allow such arrangements, and even if they do, you'll probably have to pay a tax penalty). You can also withdraw funds from your IRA if you're willing to pay the 10-percent penalty. Other retirement sources are also available.

Life Insurance Loans. Most insurance policies permit you to borrow at low rates.

Seller Financing. Homeowners will sometimes assist a buyer by offering financing, usually a first or second mortgage, renting with an option to buy, or even a wrap-around mortgage. Approximately 10

percent of today's deals are made with some type of seller financing, so tell your broker of your interest.

In a *first mortgage* the seller generally owns the home free and clear and has no mortgage which the buyer can assume. He therefore gives a fixed rate mortgage to the buyer below commercial rates. A *second mortgage*, also known as a "purchase money mortgage," usually makes up the difference between the down payment and an existing assumable mortgage. A *wrap-around* is offered when there is an existing mortgage at a low rate: So that the buyer does not have to take on a new high-rate mortgage, the seller creates the new mortgage and "wraps" it around his old mortgage. The interest rate on the new wrap-around is higher than the old one but lower than a bank mortgage. The new buyer makes monthly payments to the seller, and the seller continues paying off his old mortgage to the bank. The *rent-option* agreement lets the buyer rent for a stated length of time, at the end of which he can buy the property. In most cases a portion of his rent can be applied to the purchase price.

Most seller financing loans run five to seven years with a balloon payment due at the end. The most popular is the 80/10/10: the buyer puts down 10 percent, the seller carries 10 percent, and the lending institution 80 percent. But there are many variations, and it's well worth your time to explore the possibilities with your broker and the seller. Be sure to spell out all the details in a written document that's approved by your lawyer.

Equity Sharing. Homeownership remains elusive for many first-time buyers because they just don't have enough cash for the down payment or they lack income to cover monthly mortgage payments. A good way to overcome this stumbling block is equity sharing.

In an equity sharing arrangement cash-poor would-be buyers are matched up with investors interested either in putting up part of the down payment or in paying some of the monthly mortgage costs, in return for a share in the tax benefits and/or a percentage of the profits when the property is eventually sold. The partner who lives in the house pays the investor rent for occupying the investor's share of the house; this amount is in addition to his own share of the mortgage and maintenance. At the end of a specified time (mutually agreed upon by the investors), the owner-occupant buys out the investor's share at current market value, or the two partners sell the house. In either case, the investor recovers his original investment plus his share of the appreciation.

This arrangement is good for the buyer because he or she gets the desired home along with some tax breaks unavailable to renters. The investor likewise receives tax breaks, including depreciation write-offs. He is also assured that the property will be well cared for, since the other party in the deal has equity in the house, too. The most common source for equity sharing is a member of your family (see Chapter 9), but there are many investors interested in participating. Contact Shared Equity Specialists, Inc. (301-587-0867), the Prescott Forbes Group, Inc. (215-735-7851), or your real estate broker for a list.

In an equity sharing arrangement, there are several important factors to take into consideration. First of all, *the owner-occupant must pay a fair market rent*, based on what an outside tenant would pay minus the resident-owner's ownership share.

The investors must also decide *how they will divide the cost of improvements*. Generally the person living in the house will bear most of these costs, except for major renovations—such as putting in a pool—for which the non-resident investor generally pays a more substantial portion.

Finally, investors should be certain to *have a clause protecting each of them in case of default*. Ideally, it should be activated within 60 days of default: If one of the partners skips two payments, for example, then the other has a right to buy his share or sell the property.

Picking the Right Mortgage

With interest rates at the lowest they've been in years, mortgage mania is running wild, with thousands of homeowners applying for first-time mortgages and others rushing to refinance at lower rates. During 1986, over seven million mortgages were written. That means you must start to arrange your financing as soon as possible, since bank loan departments are swamped with paperwork.

The Fixed Rate Mortgage

Most Americans prefer the traditional 30-year fixed rate loan with rates now hovering around 10 percent. However, if you're interested in building up equity in your home more quickly, then you should look into a 15-year fixed rate loan. Rates are about one-half of a percentage point lower, but of course monthly payments are higher (see Table below).

If you're a first-time buyer, you probably cannot buy as much house with a 15-year loan as with a 30-year one.

The 15-Year Mortgage. The total interest you pay on the shorter loan is dramatically less, but there's a tradeoff—you forego possible investment income. Money spent on high monthly payments might possibly be put to better use in another investment. If you're self-disciplined and take out a 30-year loan, by investing or saving the difference in monthly payments between the 30-year loan and a 15-year loan, you could be well ahead. If you know you wouldn't save the difference and you want to build up equity faster, then a 15-year loan makes good sense. There's also another way to build up equity: On most 30-year loans you can pay ahead on the principal without penalty. So, pay as though you had a 15-year loan.

15-YEAR MORTGAGE VS. 30-YEAR MORTGAGE

($75,000 Mortgage)

	30-Year Fixed Rate at 10%	15-year Fixed Rate at 9.5%
Monthly Payment	$ 658	$ 783
Interest Cost First Year	7,481	7,023
Interest Cost Fourth Year	7,336	6,244
Mortgage Balance First Year	74,583	72,625
Mortgage Balance Fourth year	73,052	63,991
Interest Cost/Life	$161,942	65,970
Difference from 30-Year Fixed Rate		−$95,972

(Mortgage Bankers Association of America)

Here's one rule of thumb the experts suggest following: It's smarter to take a 30-year loan because it's sound economic sense to take the longest time period while interest rates are low. An exception would be if you are near retirement, in which case you might want to own your house free and clear by that date; then a 15-year loan might be preferable.

Adjustable vs. Fixed Rate. Adjustable rate mortgages are a fairly new phenomenon, for up until this decade all mortgages were "conventional"—a 20-percent down payment and the rest paid off over 30 years at a fixed rate. Then, along came "ARMs," in which the mortgage rates fluctuate with an index based on short-term rates. At this time, ARMs are an average of 1.6 percentage points lower than 30-year fixed rate loans, and 1.3 percentage points lower than 15-year fixed rate mortgages.

If you plan to live in your house less than five years and interest rates are low or going lower, an adjustable rate mortgage is probably better because you won't be locked in at a higher rate. But, if you're planning to stay a longer time, then lock in the lower fixed rate. *It is a gamble either way*, and there is no perfect solution.

If you select an ARM, make certain you get one:

- with a maximum cap of 5 percentage points over the rate you begin with.

- that has a cap on the amount the rate can go up on a year-to-year basis, usually 1 to 2 percent.

- that is tied to a Treasury-rate index, not the bank's cost of money.

Some ARMs allow you to switch to a fixed rate loan, with little or no penalty. These are rare, but worth seeking out. Ask your bank if it offers such an arrangement.

Remember, ARMs pass the burden of inflation from the bank to you. They also make future planning less certain, since your monthly mortgage payments can go up.

Caution: Errors are sometimes made when lending institutions adjust their ARMs upward. The Mortgage Bankers Association says you should insist that your bank send you a step-by-step calculation of how the new rate was reached. And, you should know what index the rate is tied to. It is probably based on a three- or five-year Treasury Bill rate, disclosed each Monday by the Federal Reserve Board or the U.S. Treasury Security Index, and based on a statistical model. Both are published in the financial pages of the newspaper and are available from your Federal Reserve Board.

If you have trouble doing your own calculations, contact Loan-Tech. For $20 this company will provide a five-year analysis of an existing ARM and its rates. Call LoanTech in Gaithersburg, MD, at 301-330-0777.

THE ADJUSTABLE RATE MORTGAGE

- **Initial Interest Rate:** Lower than fixed rate during first year; then generally rises after first adjustment period

- **Interest Rate Adjustment Period:** Rate usually adjusted once a year, but can vary

- **Interest Rate Cap:** Limits amount of increase from one adjustment period to the next

- **Lifetime Cap:** Limits total increase; some ARMs also have a floor on how low interest rate can go

- **Index:** Basis on which lending institutions establish their interest rates; usually tied to T-Bill rate or other national inflation-sensitive gauge

- **Margin:** Additional percentage points added on to the index to give the lending institution some profit

Computerized Shopping

If you suffer from borrower's anxiety (and everyone does)—that sinking feeling that a better mortgage deal may be just around the corner—you can get relief from one of the nationwide computerized services. These data bases, available at a growing number of real estate and financial firms, gather together for you a huge amount of material on various lending institutions—far more than you could ever get by dialing the banks in your area yourself.

These services vary, and some are stronger in given regions of the country than others, so it's worth your while to check them all.

You can expect to receive the following:

- annual percentage rate for each mortgage offered

- discount points offered

- closing costs charged

- details on converting an ARM to a fixed-rate loan

- assumable mortgage statistics

- qualifications a borrower must meet

- refinancing information

- evaluation of how much a borrower can afford, based on income, debts, and cash available for down payment and closing costs.

BECOME AN EXPERT

Here's a list of major computerized services:

- Compufund
  4900 Hopyard Rd.
  Pleasanton, CA 94566
  415-463-2667

- Shelternet
  200 White Plains Rd.
  Tarrytown, NY 10591
  800-822-5587

- LoanExpress
  7531 Leesburg Pike
  Falls Church, VA 22041
  703-790-3600

Also worth considering:

- Fairmont Funding
  212-967-4700

- Prudential Home Mortgage
  800-CALL-PRU

- Loan Depot
  800-USA-LOAN

Buying with a Friend

A fresh and innovative way to get into real estate if you are shy of cash (or even if you're not) is to buy with a friend. It's often a great solution for singles who can't quite swing the down payment or monthly payments on their own yet want to build up equity in the world of real estate. You don't have to be single, however, to benefit from buying with someone else. Nor do you have to be in love to "mingle," as it's called. Mingling works for live-togethers, best friends, cousins, or colleagues. The size of the group involved can vary depending upon how large a piece of property you buy and your predilection for sharing. Even co-ops and condos may be purchased by groups of more than two, although there's a greater possibility of run-ins with boards, and you can expect difficulty in obtaining financing. Regardless of the relationship between the people involved, the basics for making it work are the same. The most common and trouble-free situation is a 50-50 division of down payment, monthly mortgage payments, utilities, upkeep, taxes, and space.

To avoid surprises and pitfalls, it is essential that you draw up a written contract using a real estate lawyer with experience in mingling. The points that should be covered are:

- In whose name will the mortgage be held? Not all banks allow both parties to purchase a mortgage on one piece of property.

- How will mortgage and down payment be divided? This is very important if one person earns much more than the other.

- Title of ownership (see page 119)

- Who may live in the house in addition to the original purchasers? Children? Friends? Parents? For how long? Do they pay? Is subleasing permitted if one owner is transferred or away for several months? If one partner gets married?

- What financial arrangements will be made if one partner becomes ill, loses his or her job, or defaults on payments? One method that works is deducting the delinquent dollar amount against that person's interest in the property.

- If one partner moves out permanently, to whom can his or her share be sold?

- If one partner dies, how will his or her share and possessions be handled?

- If the financial division is uneven, how will unequal interests be handled in the eventuality that the house is sold?

- How will disagreements be resolved? Will an arbitrator be used? If so, who will pay?

Avoiding Dissolution Problems

By putting as much as possible in writing you will sidestep many issues, the most crucial of which is the question of dissolution. Each partner must be protected if the other decides to leave. Talk to your lawyer about adding two clauses to your contract.

One clause should provide each partner with a "first option" on the other's interest in the property. This enables the remaining partner to buy out the other or find a new partner. Include a fairly long notice period, three months if possible.

The second clause should call for an independent appraisal, so both partners have an equitable way to establish their dollar interest should mingling come to an end.

Property Title

The form of title is particularly crucial in mingling ownership. Review these three basic forms with your lawyer.

1) Joint Tenants: In this form if one partner dies his share automatically goes to the other. It passes outside the will and thus avoids probate. In general, each owns half the property and each takes half the tax benefits, regardless of the percentage of the property for which they have paid. In this form of ownership neither partner can leave his or her shares to anyone else (for example, to children of a former marriage, or to parents). Therefore, joint tenantship is usually recommended for married couples.

2) Tenants in Common: This form gives each tenant an undivided interest in the property, which he or she is free to sell or will to anyone they like. It is the most frequent form of co-ownership for unrelated partners, and is favored by singles who wish to leave their property to a child, friend, parent, or favorite charity. Tax benefits—mortgage interest, real estate taxes, and profits when and if the house is sold—flow to each partner. For example, if one person pays 65 percent, then he or she owns 65 percent of the property, whereas in joint tenants each owns 50 percent regardless of what percentage they paid.

3) Partnership: In this arrangement the partnership owns the property, and the individuals own shares in the partnership. It tends to be more expensive to set up than the previous two forms. The advantages are that if one partner dies it does not affect the other, and shares can be passed on to heirs. Partnership is sometimes an advisable option when individuals are buying unequal amounts of a property.

Appendix:
Mortgage-eze

Accelerated Amortization: Arrangement whereby buyer makes higher monthly payments than initially required by mortgage because he wants to reduce the amount of principal owed and/or to pay off the mortgage in a shorter time period.

Adjustable-Rate Mortgage (ARM): Mortgage with variable interest rates which are tied to an index, usually Treasury Bills.

Amortization: Gradual repayment of the *principal* of a mortgage, as opposed to the *interest*.

Assumable Mortgage: Buyer of a mortgaged home takes over the seller's original mortgage, usually at below-market rates. Normally the original lender must approve the new debtor in order to release the seller from liability.

Balloon Mortgage: Mortgage in which after a certain time period the loan must be paid in full or refinanced. Until that balloon payment is due, the borrower makes regular monthly payments, which often cover only the interest, with principal (or balloon) due when the mortgage comes due.

Blanket Mortgage: Covers an entire building or cooperative rather than separate mortgages on individual apartments.

Buydown: An incentive offered by lenders or developers to help buyers meet payments in the early years of the mortgage. Involves a reduction of interest rates for a short time or for the full mortgage period. Developer or other source subsidizes buyer's monthly mortgage payments to reduce interest rate.

Capital Appreciation: Increase in the market value of real estate over what you initially paid.

Carrying Costs: The various ongoing expenses of running a home, such as mortgage payments, real estate taxes, utilities, insurance, and repairs.

Cash Flow: Current cash return on an investment made in a piece of property.

Closing Costs: Expenses of buying property (other than down payment) which are traditionally paid when deal is closed. Include lawyer's fees, title insurance premium, survey, appraisal, inspection, mortgage application fees, and any other bank fees.

Collateral: The property that secures the loan repayment; your home or apartment is the bank's collateral on a mortgage.

Condominium: A system of ownership in which you and your neighbors each own your individual dwelling and share ownership of the common areas, such as recreation areas, hallways, elevators, pool.

Cooperative: A building consisting of two or more units in which the right to live is acquired by purchasing stock in a corporation that owns the property. You also have a proprietary lease for your individual space.

Default: Failure to meet terms of the mortgage on a piece of real estate, including not paying interest and principal when due.

Depreciation: Tax break allowing you to deduct a percentage of the cost of rental property from your taxable income. This is a reasonable allowance for the real or theoretical exhaustion, wear, and tear of property used in a trade or business.

Down Payment: Your initial cash payment on a piece of real estate.

Equity: The amount of property you own—and have paid for— outright. It is based on the fair market value of the property less any outstanding principal (*not* interest) owed.

FHA Mortgage: A low-down-payment home mortgage insured by the Federal Housing Administration. Maximum amount available varies from state to state.

Interest: The money paid for the use of money. When you borrow money from a bank or other lender, you are charged interest for use of these funds.

Leverage: Use of borrowed money to pay for part of a piece of property. If you buy a $100,000 home using $25,000 of your own cash and borrowing $75,000, your leverage is 3 to 1—i.e., you borrowed $3 for every $1 you put up.

Liquidity: How quickly an investment can be converted into cash. Common stock or shares in a money market fund are more liquid than a house or vacation time shares.

Maturity Date: Date on which the principal and interest on a mortgage are due in full.

Mortgage: Process whereby a lending institution lends you money with which to buy real estate. It must be accompanied by a legal document. The lender then has a claim against the property should you default on your loan payments.

Non-Recourse Mortgage: Mortgage in which the borrower is not personally liable. In other words, if you default on your payments, the lender's recourse is limited to recovering the property; he cannot sue you personally if the value of the real estate is less than the mortgage amount due.

Points: Payments to a lender sometimes required when you take out a mortgage. A point is equal to one percent of the amount of the mortgage and is basically an interest payment.

Prepayment: Repayment of mortgage prior to maturity. Often done to take advantage of lower interest rates through refinancing mortgage at new rate. There may or may not be a penalty.

Principal: The amount you borrow when you get a mortgage. The cost of borrowing is the *interest*.

Public Limited Partnership: An organization consisting of a general partner, who manages the deals, and limited partners, who invest money but have limited liability and are not involved in day-to-day management. Minimum investments are often as low as $1,000.

Refinancing: Prepaying your existing mortgage and replacing it with a new, sometimes larger loan, often at a lower interest rate.

Reverse-Annuity Mortgage: An annuity in place of a lump sum upon obtaining your mortgage. The mortgage need not be paid until the date of maturity. Designed especially for senior citizens.

Roll-Over Mortgage: ROMs are also known as renegotiable mortgages. After a short time, usually three to five years, the mortgage can be extended at the borrower's option for additional periods. Interest rate is renegotiated at each extension. You are gambling that interest rates will be lower in the future. Different from ARMs in that ARMs are issued for a stated period of time.

Second Mortgage: Supplementary mortgage obtained from a source other than the first mortgage bank, often from the seller, if bank first mortgage financing will not cover the cost of the home you're purchasing. It is usually subordinated to the first mortgage, so should you default, claims from the first mortgage bank would be paid first.

Shared-Equity Mortgage: Mortgage in which a third party, often a relative, contributes to the homebuyer's down payment and/or monthly payments. In exchange, the third party/investor has a share in the property's equity and in some of the tax benefits.

Title Insurance: Protection from any potential losses that arise from problems in the legal title to (right to ownership of) your property.

VA Mortgage: Home mortgage guaranteed by the Veterans Administration, generally up to $27,500. Available only to eligible veterans, it sometimes eliminates the need for a down payment.

Variable Rate Mortgage: Similar to the roll-over mortgage, except interest rate adjustments are made more frequently—generally every six months, according to a formula.

Zero-Interest Mortgage: Interest-free loan which requires a large down payment, generally one third of the purchase price. Then, payments for the remaining two thirds are made in equal installments over five to seven years. Not available at all lending institutions.